I dedicate this book to my favorite storytellers of all time, my parents, Maureen and Alexander Anstee and my grandmother, Etta May John

'If we want to see each other, it's simple, we just have to open our eyes and look, but if we want to know each other, we have to go further, dig deeper and open our vulnerable hearts. That's where the good stuff is.'

Christopher Anstee

My name is Christopher John Anstee and in the pure evidence of its magnificence, I'm going to talk to you about the intricate brilliance and beauty of life.

I am no more or less extraordinary than any other human being out there in this world. And yet, just like you, I am absolutely extraordinary in a way that no one else can be. By definition, ordinary means standard, not special, not unique or distinctive, and yet distinction is the blood that runs through the veins of this planetary spectacle called life. Being unique is the one thing that we all have in common. You could say that the very essence of life that makes us all different is the only true thing that makes us all the same. My personal conclusion is that there is not one single human being living or dead that is or ever was, simply ordinary. Therefore, it is with the greatest pleasure that I can announce that we are all extraordinary, we are all unique, we all have something to say or contribute and we all have the potential to make a difference to our own life and the lives of those around us. We are extraordinary creators, the butterflies in the most magnificent butterfly effect. Flap those wings, people – because everything we think, say, create or do will change this world in a way that only the unique I or you can change it. In a world of ever-increasing self-doubt born from society's intolerance for imperfection, too many of us lose sight of how spectacular we really are. So it's time, time to wake up, to start a revolution, to turn the tide on society. It's time to smash the spotlight that was never needed and to walk out of the shadows, blinding the world with the kind of light that shines from the inside out. The kind of light that cannot be ignored.

The most interesting people on this planet are no longer movie stars, musicians or politicians. The people we most want to observe, read about, understand and follow are the ones that have formed part of our own lives. Reality has proved to be the revolution of our entertainment. I don't mean reality TV, but true reality: our lives and the lives of the people we actually know or have known. We are now managing our own PR, we present ourselves in a show of photographs, quotes, messages and opinions. Every last one of us has the power to reach the rest of the world with a single image that reflects a single moment in our lives and to have the planet respond to that image in seconds. Most of us have hundreds of social media followers from all over the world, people that watch our lives with interest, yet these are people that we will never know. Our behaviour has changed; we are no longer content with being spectators to a small number of people who command the stage. We now hold our own spotlight, we are all on the stage and we all have an audience, should we wish to invite them in.

Some people have said that this is a sign of reductive times. I disagree. To me, the way in which we as a people have responded to social media is the greatest experiment in human behaviour that has ever taken place. And this experiment has confirmed that no matter who you are, where you're from or what you do, your world and your story is a true celebration of life and people want to hear about it, watch it and celebrate it with you. It is inspiring to me that the lives of the many that live in normal houses, in normal communities are no longer assumed to be grey. Instead, they are known to be as colourful, thought- provoking and as celebrated as the life of an affluent celebrity, and in truth maybe more colourful, because the colour is familiar, reachable and reflective of who we are.

Through the simple art of storytelling, amplified by the power of the media platforms now available, I believe there is a great opportunity for us all to revolutionise the way we communicate. With our own stories we can cross the man-made barriers of class and embrace the variety in different cultures. Words and images are wonderful at creating moments of exposure, and with exposure we can breed tolerance. This is simply about storytelling, the understated, immeasurable power of sharing our own, real stories. This is simply recognition that we have started to wake up to the extraordinary ordinary world around us and have stopped looking to those on pedestals to provide the sparkle. In this respect I think we are living in the most exciting times, times that bring great challenges but also boundless potential for human connection.

So this is my story. My little book filled with stories, poems and memories. It is an account of parts of my life for anyone that wants to read it. One way of thinking about this book is that it's a selection of treasure, treasure from the heart and mind that I have written for those that I love and those people that love me – brilliant, extraordinary, exceptional real people. I owe my desire to tell stories to my storytelling heroes: my parents and grandparents. Growing up, I was blessed with tales of days gone by and experiences that people shared at a time before I existed. Those stories will always stay in my heart. If we don't share our story, then it is lost forever. There is such a deep richness in all life, no matter how very simple we believe it to be, that it should be preserved. Wouldn't it be wonderful to pick up a book that gave us a window into the lives of our ancestors or earlier generations, an account or biography in their own words? I want to start a revolution of literature, and if I can inspire one other person to write their story, then I will have achieved something with this book. In a heartbeat the very short list of natural biographies will start to grow and by opening the doors into ordinary extraordinary life, we as people will grow with it.

I share the sentiments of the great Charlie Chaplin in that I don't believe that you should have to explain anything creative in order for your audience to understand it. However, this short book aims to place poetry in context with my memories and stories of the life that may have inspired those poems. The hunt for the true depth of this poetry and the potential for personal interpretation, I will leave to you.

What I have created with the help of an exceptionally gifted illustrator, Barbra Anna Gomez, is a short book about life, a celebration of an ordinary, extraordinary but very simple life: my life. I hope you like it.

Chapters

The Happy Tramp

From the hills a lad was born
With bright blue eyes and sprightly form
He wouldn't sail the ship of fools
He couldn't play by others' rules

From very young he loved to dream
To look offshore, to swim the stream
He loved his roots but couldn't stay
Adventure called him far away

From a life so full of love
He searched for soul, the whitest dove
He never sang a tune for long
He hadn't found the perfect song

Happiness he sought with might
One day he knew he'd see its light
Inside true love would shine a lamp
To walk beside the happy tramp

The Butch Kid & The Iron Lady

I don't remember what day it was, the time of year or even what I was doing before or after this moment, but I'm about to share with you my very earliest memory.

I was sat at a large rectangular dining table that looked out over the small yard at the back of our house. It was a high gloss veneer kind of table, the kind that you could almost slip off while elbow resting if you weren't careful. There was a trickle of lazy rain running down the old sash window and I could see the dark cobbles of the yard outside shine and almost sparkle under the rain that showered the hard ground and the tall, overbearing grey garden wall.

The sitting room was small and dark and the table had been pushed up against the window to create as much space as possible. The grey and yellow floral print wallpaper provided the only colour in an otherwise grey day. Rain and grey skies were not unusual in the mountains of the Welsh Valleys, and that day was no different. Dinner was being prepared by my mother, who was huffing and puffing over the cooker, while my father was patiently trying to get me to write my name without me stealing a glance at his copy to remind me of the letters and their order. Our house was never quiet. In fact, I recall my mum shouting on three or four occasions for my two older brothers to come down for dinner with little success and the TV blaring in the background even though nobody was watching it. My brothers' hesitation to appear for dinner was because almost always when my mother first called us for dinner, dinner was in fact not ready at all. 'Dinner is ready' was frequently translated into 'Dinner is actually going to be ready in ten minutes, but that won't stop me shouting once a minute for the next nine of those ten.' In the final minute the tone and volume of the call to action escalated swiftly before reaching its final red alert status of 'If you don't come down right now, I am sending your father up'. Now dinner was ready!

As part of the usual pre-dinner juggling act my mother was also desperately trying to clear the table, which was covered in reams of used white paper that I had been writing on. My dad was giving that good old Welsh response, 'Now in a minute,' to buy us more time, and much to my mam's frustration it was working. I had tried so many times and refused to give up, so I went on, as did my dad's patience and my mam's momentary lack of it. Chr – ist – opher An – st – ee. Chris – topher Anstee. Christopher Anstee. I did it; I finally did it. I did it not just once but at least twenty or thirty times. With each successful attempt the praise diminished, as you would expect, but I was 'clever'. Those were my father's words and while he may never have believed it, on that day I listened to everything he said. Even as a small child I had an appalling appetite to argue a point or to defy my father but on this occasion we were in full and final agreement. For weeks I would write my name on anything that would take the ink, in fact the newspaper edging in every house I went to was often patterned with my new skill and if anyone asked my name, it was no longer spoken, oh no! That was so yesterday, from now on it would be written and pointed at with a generous, self-congratulating smile.

Having mastered my name, the world was now my oyster. On my fifth birthday, another significant event occurred: I became the proud owner of my first front-loading washing machine. In case you were thinking that must be a subsidiary event that was a part of the build-up to a more impressively significant event or gift, then I must be clear, the washing machine was both impressive and significant to this strange but ecstatic five-year-old and was by far the greatest of all accomplishments in his little life to date.

It was late September, but the sun was shining and I wasn't in school. My grandmother was coming to see me, and my mother had organised a birthday party for later that day. Good times. I have no recollection of what was once inside my beautiful washing machine – a gift of some kind I'm sure – but that had now been placed to one side to make way for the greatest gift of all. So with scissors, plasticine, felt-tip pens and some careful supervision, the once-empty box that had been destined for the bin was transformed into a state of the art automatic washing machine. There were wash selections, a fully operational door, a detergent hatch and coloured indicators that would tell me when the cycle was finished. I was so excited by my new creation I remember sitting on the front garden wall waiting for my grandmother to turn the corner at the bottom of our street – I needed to tell her about it as soon as possible. We lived in a long terraced street built during the coal industry heyday. The houses were all built from the same grey quarried stone and were all connected together on an ever so gradual incline that sloped south towards the crest of the hill. Every house was a slightly different shade of colour around the flat, heavy window frames and on one side of the street there were no front gardens, just doors leading directly onto the grey paving. We, however, were on the other side, the posh side. Not only did our side of the road have elevated front gardens with steps, my family had a semi-detached house, so in Aldergrove Road we were practically aristocracy.

The house itself was located in a small village called Porth, the Welsh word for gate. The town was called 'gate' because that is exactly what it was. Porth sat at the entrance to two separate valleys, a larger valley called Rhondda Fawr and a smaller one known as Rhondda Fach. We lived on the mountain that was positioned right in the middle of them both. It was a deep valley, and on dark winter days the height of the mountains would cast a gloomy shadow over the small runs of uniform houses below, but in the spring and summer the mountains transformed into something so very different. Out of the grey came the grazing fields of lush green, carpeted in deep purple heather. The lambs would bounce and the scattering of wild flowers would dance in the summer breeze to shake and share their sweet fragrance.

A little further up the mountain from our house, my dad had a field where a few horses were kept along with a couple of pigeon sheds that once belonged to my grandfather. Going there always felt like an adventure as a kid, as was trying to avoid the odd roaming ram and the occasionally irritated horse that always moved a little faster than my small legs would have liked. I think I spent most of the time being carried by my dad in a bid to keep me alive and my limbs intact, either that or it was my preferred method of travel and let's face it my dad did have much bigger legs than me and the view from his shoulders was always so much better. I used to like to walk up to the highest point and peer across the mountains and south down the valleys imagining that my favourite cartoon, *Cities of Gold* was just around the corner. I clearly watched too many cartoons and my imagination was far too powerful for its own good but I was very small then, so being silly was officially acceptable. What actually lay immediately beyond wasn't in fact a mystical, wonderful place made of gold, but Pontypridd. What was in my imagination was so much prettier! Pontypridd was the nearest large town, much bigger than Porth, and compared to Porth it was practically cosmopolitan. It had a few coffee shops, a market and it had been blessed with a Marks & Spencer's department store, which delivered the only magic and sparkle that the small town had to offer. Having said that, we mustn't forget that it was also the hometown of our very own Sir Tom Jones. It's not unusual for people from these parts to remember him being a young man about the town before he hit the big time. Did you see what I did there? Both my mum and dad recall him being at weekend dance nights all those years ago and my mum specifically remembers dancing with Tom Jones on more than one occasion. He clearly wasn't as good a dancer as my dad, it appears. Just as well I say.

The absolute highlight of the view from the field had to be the beautiful red coal mine towers and the pithead wheels that still remained as part of the heritage mining museum. The bright red structures stood very proud against the tall green trees that surrounded them and it was a constant reminder of our history and what had actually created this little community so many years before.

Coal has always felt like such a harsh word to me. The term 'Welsh Gold' is more appealing but almost gives the sedimentary rock too much kudos. Despite the communities it raised and the history it created, it's a word I associate with too much adversity. Many times as a child and as an adult I have tried to imagine the days of the working mines based on the stories my grandfather would tell me. His stories would conjure up images of tired men walking the cobbled streets, with soot-covered faces, desperate to wash, eat and rest. I imagined resentment and struggle in the men and fear in the wives and mothers that would watch their husbands and sons disappear down the old terraced streets to a job filled with so much danger. It's almost ironic that the very thing that kept them cold and awake underground during the long dark days was the very thing that kept them warm and cosy during the short restful nights. I don't imagine the valleys in colour back then, I imagine them to be grey and dark like the soot.

By the time I was a boy the valleys were full of colour and the landscape was beautiful, but that came at a cost. Our communities were in decline and the mines were closing all around us. Industry had started to fail and the land and the air had started to breathe and regenerate. Maybe Mother Nature was the only real winner back then.

I grew up at a time when the politics of coal dominated the headlines. I remember looking at the TV and seeing poverty and anger. The miners' strike of 1984–85 was probably the worst industrial dispute in UK history, a dispute initiated in protest of the action taken by Margaret Thatcher's administration to reduce subsidies. I also grew up watching my grandfather's health suffer at the hands of coal. My grandfather, John John, started work in the mines as a young teenage boy and paid the price eventfully with his life as he lost his battle with emphysema and dust when I was just ten years old. I often would sit opposite him and watch him struggle to do the thing that most of us take for granted more than anything else. Sometimes when he would speak to me it would use more breath than he had to give and sometimes he would smile, and I knew that was easier than speaking. So you see for me coal was much more bitter than it could ever be sweet and as we lost a great man, the industrial world fought to keep alive the very thing that had killed him. My first view of world politics at that time felt in some ways like a baptism by fire, it was laced with hate, pain and fear, and as the miners fought for the sake of their families and not for the love of coal, another horror story was unfolding before my very impressionable young eyes.

The other raging nightmare stealing the headlines under Thatcher was the campaign to prevent AIDS and the concurrent targeting of the homosexual community. Little did I know that these dark topics were in some way provoking a strange alliance between lesbian women, gay men and the South Wales mining community. Lesbian and Gays Support the Miners (LGSM) became an actual thing, and as a result of the government administration sequestering the funds of the National Union of Mineworkers, the LGSM twinned themselves directly with communities to get the charity funds straight to the people. The members of LGSM were mostly young, confident and proud, armed with a resilience that can only come from living through your own struggle, your own cause or your own battle with the world. They identified with the struggles of the miners and worked tirelessly to raise funds that they would deliver by hand directly into the middle of the failing communities.

In the South Wales Valleys at that time, it was not okay to be gay. Yes, there were one or two men that had the guts to be openly gay at that time, but despite having small circles of friends, who were usually women, it really wasn't okay. I recall one guy who had come out and who used to come into my mam's pub. He had an unconvincing air of outward confidence about him, but his own father, who was also a regular at the pub, would often dismiss his existence or fire abuse in his direction. I remember that some of his father's friends would taunt him with school yard name calling for the entertainment of those around them in the bar and I used to despair at the thought that bullying didn't stop just because you had left school. My mother would tell me that his father wanted nothing to do with him because he was gay, and hearing about that rejection was terrifying to me. Ashamed and disgusted with his own son because he was born with the same capacity to love but with a sexual preference that was different to his own. You would think from the disgust and disappointment this man showed it was almost as if his son had made a terrible choice! When in fact our deepest truth about who we are is a realisation, never a choice, not really. In fact, the only choice that young gay people had at that time was whether to be truthful or not about who they were. Every one of these young men and women that stood up and took the truthful road less travelled made the pathway just that little bit easier for those that followed, and I will always respect that, having observed the very real social punishment that comes from living a truth out loud.

It's so easy now to look back at the blatant intolerance of the past with judgement and disgust, but is that any fairer than the intolerance itself? Isn't it all a case of trying to understand each other better? It's inconceivable to ever justify hatred and bulling but those actions are very different to widespread, passive ignorance born from never knowing any other way. These were small communities where generation after generation had followed tradition, where no role models existed to provide a different way of viewing what was such a small world. These were good people, hardworking people, and a people with the deepest hearts. Sometimes we just have to accept that for people to change their outlook, someone has to be the first to stand up and give them a different view of the landscape, a view they never knew existed. So, you see for the narrow-minded

Welsh communities at that time, it was so difficult to accept help from a group of people that were no more accepted or tolerated within their community than the Iron Lady herself, but that is exactly what they did, despite their prejudice. Much more significant than the acceptance of their support was the Welsh community's acceptance of them as human beings, human beings united in a struggle to survive.

In those small communities, walls were broken down and intolerance became tolerance and even respect. It wasn't pride that was swallowed to make that alliance, it was ignorance, and in this case ignorance was definitely not and never would be bliss. If you have never seen the film *Pride*, then you really should, it is an amazing story and more than that, it's an amazing true story.

So the political world was covered in dark clouds. And though at the time I was too young to consider the real long-term impact of what the politicians and news presenters were saying, I was old enough to digest the feelings of the world around me in response to it. To me back then the news was another form of entertainment, but while I was sure I didn't like Margaret Thatcher I used to be captivated by her, especially when she would stand outside No. 10 and give a strong, defiant speech through the TV and straight into my little world. The content wasn't important – not to me, anyway – but she was a strong woman, and I liked and respected that. I guess a speech from the Iron Lady was my earliest guilty pleasure and believe me, if you came from where I come from, then that really was a guilty pleasure you would never admit to.

So let's get back to my birthday and September 1980. My mother sat with me on the front garden wall as we waited patiently for my grandmother to turn that corner and wave. My mam was popping in and out of the house to check on whatever it was she was cooking at the time, but I was keeping watch and refused to move. I think I thought that if I wasn't watching then my grandmother wouldn't come. My mam was too busy really to be sat with me as I dangled my little legs in the air, keeping watch, but she sat with me anyway. When I was younger there was nothing I loved more than being around my mother, I was the proverbial mummy's boy, and the title never bothered me, in fact I could never understand the insult. If I wasn't pretending to cook with vegetable scraps she would be cutting or pretending to be a doctor operating on the cauliflower stems that fell onto the worktop, then I was eager to polish and vacuum. I'm not sure if I loved being a little cleaner or I just wanted to be like my mam, I just remember being a happy little boy, happiest when I was following around after my mother. I was my mam and dad's little shadow, and to this day, they are the only shadows that I can ever remember wanting to be in.

My Fair Lady

For twinkling eyes and a tiny heart
The light of love did forever shine
With tiny steps, from stop to start
The strongest hand holding on to mine
My rising sun and my kiss goodnight
My safety blanket to hold me tight

For curious joy and bundles of go
A protection so mighty it never would flee
The boundless believer who never said no
To the boy in her shadow, in her shadow was me
My arms to run to at the end of the day
My cwtch to remind me that all was okay

For the ambitious explorer so eager to grow
The hand on the shoulder with wisdom and sight
From the slips to the slides to the ebbs and the flow
The endless forgiver, the torch in the night
My strength and my steel always walking with me
My inspiration to be the best man I could be

From happy and chirpy to moods with great flair
A beautiful bond that shines bright like no other
The Tom and the Cherries a laughter to share
The blessing of gold a son's love for his mother
My wind and my sail with the deepest devotion
My reason for surviving the storms in my ocean

From old movies and glamour, a star in disguise
In old pictures a beauty that couldn't compare
A wondrous kindness with no boundary or size
In a smile was a warmth wrapped in sparkle and flair
My shimmering icon from first breath as her baby
My own Audrey Hepburn, my mam, my Fair Lady

From the truest of eyes and the biggest heart
This glorious love will forever shine
Though life can conspire to stop and to start
My hand is in hers and hers is in mine
I am forever her son and her lamp in the night
She is forever my mam, my most beautiful light

I loved being with my dad, but my dad was the disciplinarian and said no, more often that I would have liked! 'No' was a word that I struggled with as a child; a restriction, a thought-provoking statement that often meant me having to reconsider my cunning plans. I needed to get older to realise how much I liked my dad. I always loved him but as I got older I realised that I didn't just love him because he was my father; I actually loved him because I respected where he had come from and I looked up to his gentle, content nature and could see the depth of his heart. When we were kids, however, he wouldn't take any messing about, there was no room for a child diva in his house! I had the typical good cop bad cop scenario, but even though I would hold onto my mother's apron strings to be saved from the world, I always knew deep down that the bad cop was never really that bad – in fact the bad cop was probably a 'bad' bad cop.

Some of my favourite bad cop fails were when Dad would let me escape the sentence of an 'early to bed' school night in exchange for my promise to go to sleep on the sofa with no TV peeping. He would lay on the front edge and I would tuck myself in behind him facing the back of the sofa. That was my way of making a statement about how serious I really was and that I had every intention of going to sleep as per the arrangement. That was of course absolutely not my intention, but rather stage one of my mission to deceive my father and secure another hour in the land of the living. I would lay there for maybe ten to fifteen minutes, biding my time until it seemed that enough time had passed that a discreet twist and turn by me would almost be expected. The final part of stage one was the eventual full body turn and the burying of my face in my dad's shoulder. This was an art in itself, because my face had to land in exactly the right place to allow for stage two to actually work. Failure would mean more fidgeting, and one fidget too many could always bring the risk of irritation leading to capture and banishment to bed! So, on to stage two. Stage two would involve the discreet popping open of one eye and a strain to look over my father's shoulder at the TV to assess what exactly I was missing. This was equally as delicate as stage one, and made more so by the teasing realisation that I was almost there. However, eye popping was in itself irritating and could only be managed in short bursts, which ran the risk of catching my dad's 'un-popping' eye. Rescue mode was always to twitch my nose, and yawn as if simply adjusting my sleep position, and at worst that would result in an inquisitive but softly threatening 'are you peeping?' I never replied of course. I was far too busy sleeping. All this hard work was essential in the build-up to stage three. Stage three was the brave stage, and this involved actually speaking. It was like those moments in later life when you're about to tell someone you love them for the first time and you know you are going to say it but time stops and tumbleweeds appear to be gliding across the floor as you enter a tormented state of waiting as that perfect millisecond continues to elude you! This wasn't quite that dramatic, but nonetheless it was dramatic enough for this little performer. 'Dad, I'm not comfy and you're squashing me a bit, can I lay in front please?' There it was! The mic would hit the deck and the crowd would go wild... Success depended on the delivery – it had to be said in a traumatised, tired, sleepy voice, the kind of voice that implied, 'If you make me go upstairs to bed I will wake up and never get back to sleep, but if you just let me sleep on the outside of the sofa then I will sleep like a sleep-deprived turtle in hibernation.' The final stage had mixed results, but I definitely won more than I lost, so with a tiny flicker of my dad's approval I would roll over to the front of the sofa, the front row seat, and from here I could peep uninterrupted at the TV for as long as I wanted... just like a boss. It's such a shame that the exhausting masquerade to get there always sent me fast asleep within moments of winning the prize. It was only a few years ago that I realised that my father probably knew exactly what it was that I was doing all along, in fact we probably shared the same plan, only my father won and I more often than not, lost. All that fuss and drama for less than generous results! Although, it wasn't all a waste of time. I did get carried to bed most evenings and ended up being tucked into bed with a gentle hair ruffling, which I knew was my father saying, I love you.

The Man That Stood In Front Of Me

The smallest I will ever be, before the teenager came to be
In a train just you and me, a coffee shop, chocolate and tea
On your shoulders I would smile, childhood lasted just a while
Strong hands held on to me so tight, the safest place of all

One yesterday I didn't see, the man that stood in front of me
I never stopped to take the time, to understand your heart
Seasons passed and I grew tall, independence loomed, my heart
grew small
Always the one to tell me no, I didn't understand at all

I grew hungry to find me, something you could already see
Tomorrow was about the man, who didn't know the way
Lessons learned and time has seen, a story of what has always been
In the story you were there with me, always at my side

I see you now in you and me, I the apple you the tree
The patience of the strongest heart, I see, I understand
One day I hope to be like you, contented to love just like you do
Contented and so full of peace, for all that life can bring

You're loved by all that also see, the man that stood in front of me
Your gentle kindness now adored, by the children at your side
The lucky ones that share your light, the happy day, the playful
night
From a distance I now smile, for the days when that was me

So never has there ever been, a man so happy to be me
A man because you loved me, from the bottom of your heart
Time can fly and days be had, and in all of them you'll be my dad
Your son can only wish to be, the man that stood in front of me.

Anyway, let's wrap up the story of my fifth birthday. It was my actual birthday, and I was sitting in the sun with my mother after an exhausting morning of pretending to clean the house, my grandmother was coming to see me and I was going to have a party with all of my friends and a red polka dot Mickey Mouse birthday cake that very evening. Oh, and I now owned a washing machine that I was so excited to use, I could barely contain myself. Life didn't get much better in my world. I know what you're thinking… butch kid!

Finally, the moment arrived and Etta appeared around at the top of the hill and waved. I wanted to run down the street to meet her, but I wasn't allowed so I just waved like a crazy person until eventually she made it up the front garden steps, across the path and in through the front door. There were a few people in my life that I loved enough to bust and Etta May John was one of them. My grandmother, who my brothers and I called Nanna, was a small, dainty lady with the most wonderful smile. She was always dressed neatly, with rosy cheeks from the dusting of blusher, and her hair a bunch of tight silver curls that she would perm once a month. I would spend hours sat with my grandmother on sleepovers, listening to wartime stories and looking through old photographs while being fed a constant stream of my favourite foods, including her unbeatable homemade apple pie. My grandparents' home was a sweet little house but in my topsy-turvy imagination it was like stepping into a Tardis that became Charlie's chocolate factory. For me it was a special place filled with stories, laughter and things I loved to play with that I probably shouldn't have been playing with at all. It smelt like apples, chocolate and fizzy lemonade and it was always warm and cosified (which I know isn't a word; it should be because that is exactly how I would describe my grandparents' place). It was my hideaway at the top of the tree-lined hill that led out of our village, a magic place where for me everything was always just perfect. The house sat in a small quiet cul-de-sac not far away from where we lived. In spring the street would be lined with the most beautiful blossom trees and I remember thinking that the petals looked like wedding confetti when they eventually fell each year, sprinkling the road with pastel pinks and whites. It was almost like the Hindu festival of colour but with petals and not powder (and without the mess afterwards). I'm sure my vivid, imagination-fuelled memories are brighter than the reality, but it was without question very beautiful. The house had a roaring coal fire that would crackle and smoke with a distinctive soft, sooty smell. The smell was all embracing as was the entertainment value of simply watching it. Once in a while I would have the job of going out to the coal house with a bucket to replenish the fire, one coal at a time. It was kind of like being picked to do the milk bottle run at infants' school but much more grown up and much more rewarding. My gran would sit in a tall leather armchair in front of the fire and I would sit opposite the fire, laid out on the sofa, facing the TV like a little lord. The carpet was floral, with a deep pile that was soft underfoot, and the curtains at the front and back were changed to reflect the seasons. I never really understood that, but it made me smile. Either we naturally shared a sense of humour or Nanna gave me my sense of humour. I'm not sure which it was but a night in on the sofa listening to my grandmother's warm chuckle as we watched a Laurel and Hardy movie was a priceless gift. In fact, when I look back, every moment I spent with her was priceless.

On the day of my fifth birthday there was another milestone: the first piece of music I ever owned, my first seven-inch vinyl. I apparently loved 'Imagine' by John Lennon and would often glide around the house to the melody like some crazed child ballerina, so to encourage said gliding, 'Imagine' is exactly what my grandmother had bought me. It had a plain vintage white cover and the Apple Records emblem was showing through the circular window. It's a tune that has formed part of the soundtrack to my life and to this day is one of my favourite songs. On that day I must have listened to it a hundred times as I pirouetted through the house in between the cardboard washing machine spin cycles. However, when it was first handed to me I was apparently rather busy. If memory serves me correctly, my grandmother had only just given me my present and had barely taken off her cardigan when I had whipped up the cardigan and her scarf and stuffed it with haste into the washing machine along with every coat and scarf that was hanging under the staircase. I didn't wash the record of course, that was placed carefully on the record player for later. I was very pleased with myself and in my little head I was very proud of the new Anstee Jnr laundry service.

I'm not sure anyone shared that view after retrieving the clothes a few hours later. It appears that if you stuffed clothes into a small, cramped space with little in the way of finesse or care, they would actually emerge more than a little creased and in desperate need of a good ironing. I was unable to help with that, of course – ironing wasn't for butch kids, after all!

The Great Foundations

Growing up I had a real grandmother as well as my lovely Aunty Nan. Aunty Nan was my mum's aunt but we had adopted her as our other grandmother. Aunty Nan was the down to earth, larger than life, bubbly, lovely, chirpy, cwtchy gran that was always there in the thick of it; shouting at us for making too much noise, meeting us from school, cleaning our ears with her handkerchief and generally being a big old bossy softy. She was a larger lady with a round, happy face and white curly hair that had turned a soft tone of yellow at the fringe due to a lifetime of cigarettes, but most of all Aunty Nan was defined by being the life and soul of wherever she happened to be. She loved to laugh, to smoke, to have a cheeky drink and never ever missed the bingo in the local hall. She lived a simple life, in a very small terraced house further up the valleys, but she was loved by everyone who knew her and while she didn't have much in terms of money, she had a heart of solid gold.

As a young lady Aunty Nan was the wealthy wife of Dick Cronin and together they lived with greater means than most of the community around them. They were the first people with a car in their neighbourhood and would often be the house that people would visit to request a loan. Aunty Nan had bright, beautiful clothes and it was easy to imagine her in her younger years about the town, I imagine her back then as an outward expression of what I came to know as her almost flamboyant spirit. Aunty Nan had a privileged start in her adult life and while she was never less than happy, Dick deprived her of the one thing she had always wanted: children. Despite their comfortable financial position, sadly life didn't bring them lasting happiness. Dick died at a young age leaving a relatively young, widowed Nan Cronin still with most of her life ahead of her. Over the years Aunty Nan made her way through the wealth that Dick had left her, mostly due to her appetite for living it up and partially due to her giving nature that unfortunately attracted a handful of supposed friends that would take advantage of her kindness. Despite her life-changing setback, Nan Cronin had served a greater purpose, one that in a way gave her the thing she'd always wanted. When my real grandmother's health failed, Nan Cronin stepped in to help raise my mother.

When my mother was just a few years old my grandmother developed tuberculosis and was hospitalised for almost two years. I remember as a child working tirelessly through my grandparents' photo collection, asking them to tell me all about the faces on the pictures. There was one photo of my mother as a little girl that my grandmother would always take from me and hold for just a few minutes. I remember asking her one day why she always looked so sad when she held that photo. She said, 'This is the picture I held in my hands and cried myself to sleep with every night while I was away from your mother in hospital. She was so beautiful, she was my little girl.' My mother often used to doubt the depth of my grandmother's love for her because she missed out on her early life, but to me it was always abundantly clear that my grandmother loved her as much in her older years as she had loved the little girl in the picture all of those years before. I have come to learn that sometimes we are too close to our insecurities to see them clearly, and so we have to harvest perspective from those we trust. My mother was too close to her own insecurities to see just how loved she really was and I have spent a lifetime trying to bring that to life for her. The true crush point for my mother was the fact that she had never heard her parents tell her that they loved her, yet I saw them say it in a hundred different ways. The power of the words 'I love you' is easy to dismiss if you are blessed enough to hear it, but in the absence of those words we are left to search for evidence and proof that the truth is simply unspoken. I made it a principle in my life to never leave the words unspoken and yet to only say it when I felt it from the deepest part of my soul. Sometimes it is still a difficult thing to say for me, and I will never know why, maybe because it exposes the truest part of our souls, and maybe that vulnerability relinquishes our heavily guarded emotional control. Maybe saying 'I love you' from a place of pure truth, sets us free, helps us grow, and maybe we give a little piece of ourselves away every time we say it. Even as I write this, I am suddenly aware of the people in this world whom I truly love and yet I have never told them. Time to call off the guards and relinquish a little of that control I think.

The hospital that my gran stayed at was in a place called Sully, a coastal spot in the Vale of Glamorgan. The modernist sanatorium overlooked the sea, which felt like a bittersweet gift for those that stayed in the otherwise haunting accommodation. The hospital was an imposing, white, art deco style building that looked like an old

Miami hotel that had been destined to feature in a black and white horror movie. The long tree-lined driveway gave way to the suffocating yet perfectly symmetrical east and west wings, that reached out to bring you in through its central rotating doors. It was a place I heard many stories about, and a place that I never once felt the need to visit other than through my grandmother's memories.

My grandfather had to work long hours to keep the home going and in between work had to travel many miles to visit my grandmother as often as he could. He had no choice but to give his little girl, my mother, into the care of her grandmother and Aunty Nan. Nan Cronin emotionally adopted my mother in those early years and in her heart I believe that she always looked upon my mother as her own child. By default I suppose we became her grandchildren. One thing is for sure, while she didn't end up a wealthy old lady, she did end her days a much-loved part of our family. I often see my Aunty Nan in aspects of my mum's character and it makes me smile because she was very special to us. So I guess we had two grandmothers and my mum had two very special and two very different mums. The last time I saw Aunty Nan she was sat in the sitting room at our house and she had emptied her whole handbag into her lap for a sort out. She used to do this all the time and yet a few days later it would be full to busting once again. It was a small brown clip bag that bulged, so full she could barely clip it shut. If she wasn't sorting out the whole bag, she would empty her purse onto her lap and sort out her change, ensuring she had enough for bingo and cigarettes. As she was getting up to leave that day she kissed me and said, 'Give me a kiss, you never know what's around the corner.' That night she died peacefully in her sleep. My brother identified the body and said, 'She was so peaceful, just curled up asleep.' And that is exactly how she deserved to leave this world, a world a little bit warmer because of Nan Cronin.

As people came into my life in later teenage and adult years, I have often thought to myself that they missed out by not knowing Aunty Nan, but we knew her, and we were so blessed to have her in our lives. If I close my eyes, I can still remember seeing her happy face waiting for me at the school gates. I would run over and grab her hand out of sheer excitement, excitement to be going home and excited that Aunty Nan was there to take me.

By the very nature of the fact that I had a father I also had another biological grandmother, though we never met. My dad's mum, Annie Eirwen Anstee, died suddenly in her early forties due to an untreatable heart condition. My dad remembers walking five miles through heavy snowstorms and bitter cold to get home to his father when he had heard his mum had passed away. The journey across the Welsh winter valleys and up the steep slopes of the mountains would have been torturous for anyone on any occasion, but on that night, it was a son making his way home to his family under the dark cloud of losing his mam. He recalls the blizzard's bitter and sharp winds beating against his face as he threw his weight against the wind at 2 a.m. that morning, desperate to get home, desperate to understand. Earlier that night my dad had intended to call in to see his mum but had changed his mind at the very last minute. I can tell that that decision still hurts him whenever he tells the story, but how could he ever have known what was going to happen that night. Even if he hadn't changed his mind, it may have already been too late.

Annie, who was known by her neighbours and friends as Nancy, was a shy, hardworking, and gentle housewife who lived with my grandfather, Alexander, way up on the mountain in a steep terraced cobbled street that looked out over the vast expanse of mountainous farmland. She worked hard and had very little, always finding ways to make food stretch so that none of the five children went without. My dad was one of six but only five of them grew beyond infancy after the loss of a baby called Francis to cot death. My dad recalls my grandmother's life being hard but devoted, devoted to making the best of the hand she had been dealt for herself and the little humans around her, who she loved so dearly.

In Wales in the 40s and 50s life was tough. People washed in tin tubs, used a toilet in an outdoor shed and lived on rations. Homes were basic, with little to nothing in the form of luxury. Some were better off than others but generally people were poor. The houses had been built specifically to accommodate the rapid growth of the coal industry and even today if you drive around the Welsh valleys you can see the separation of wealth and status from back in those boom days. The houses range from tiny and many to boastful but few. You could look at a house and know at a glance if it was a worker, a supervisor or a manager's home. Even within that one category of manager you could see the seniority of management in the architecture. My Dad's parents were one of the poorer families and life was hard.

I used to often think about my dad's mum because she had always been a mystery to me. Even as an adult I still find myself asking questions about her and I like to think that I have created a picture of what she was like in my mind. When I think of Annie Anstee, I think of a kind, gentle but strong lady and even though I never did meet her, from what I now know I am still proud to be able to say I am her grandson. I will always wish I had known her from more than just my dad's memories, and if there had ever been a person that I wish had written a book about their life the way I am doing now, it would have been Annie Eirwen Anstee, my grandmother.

My grandfathers were both around when I was a child but I never spent as much time with them, mainly because they both died when I was relatively young, which feels like such a long time ago now. Time has a wicked tendency to edit our memories any way that it can, and though we lose things, the silver lining is that time usually filters out the forgettable moments and keeps the good stuff. I think I have just that in my memory of my grandfathers. My dad's dad was always old and frail in appearance when I was a kid, he never spoke much and when he did it was usually to my dad, but I used to like to go and see him nonetheless. He had an old portly dog called Togo who didn't do much more than breathe and eat but I always recall him sat at my grandfather's feet, like a big fat furry foot warmer. They always looked like they had been stuck together for a lifetime, like old friends. My grandfather was named Alexander, just like his dad before him and so it goes without saying that is why my dad was also blessed with the traditional name of Alexander Anstee. Why not? Don't fix what isn't broken, I say. Like most men of a certain age in the Welsh Valleys, my grandfather was a pigeon fancier. Now let me clear something up for those that don't know: a pigeon fancier doesn't fancy pigeons! That would of course be more than a little bit wrong, right? So, my grandfather kept two large pigeon sheds that sat on the mountain opposite their house. The sheds looked like someone had contracted them from thrown away pieces of mismatched wood, and that is probably exactly how they were constructed. I used to imagine them as grand pigeon hotels and I expect that the pigeon community at the time thought them to be boastfully luxurious. There were little decks they could rest on in the sun, a large communal bird bath on the floor for bathing, a little nook where they would all meet to scoff their fresh seed and each pigeon had their own little shelf or guest room as I liked to consider them. I mean on the scale of bird houses, a pigeon shed really was the Burj Al Arab. So as I was explaining, my grandfather would train said pigeons to race in competitions, yes that is what you read, they would train and compete in real, actual competitions! It absolutely stunned me as a child that I, a relatively intelligent little being, could get lost in Tesco and have to run screaming to the nearest available adult (yes, it happened more than once), and yet these dumb but sometimes beautiful looking birds could be placed in a basket, driven hundreds of miles and released to fly all the way back home on the wind. Shocking and magnificent, don't you think? Not only would they fly home, they would do so with such speed that my grandfather's pigeons often did win major competitions. They actually had Pigeon Award Evenings, where the men who had competed in that year would win large sums of money and pick up enormous trophies for their sideboards. The wives would get all dressed up and there would be drinks and dinner prior to the awards going out, like the Oscars but for pigeons. Well, kind of. Amazement and wonder aside, I did love sitting on the deck of my grandfather's pigeon cot with my legs dangling over the edge, looking out across the fields and into the sky waiting for a grey speck to appear. I always had a talking issue, however, and so would often get told off for talking and putting off the birds! My memories of sunny days and running around with the chickens and the dogs in my grandfather's field are now faded, just like the reductive world of the pigeon fancier, but the memories I do have are special ones.

My other grandfather was very different to my dad's dad, my mam's dad was tall, bold and he loved to talk – and talk loud! He used to give me money from a brown leather wallet that snapped open at the top like it would take your fingers off if they ever got caught in there, and he used to say, 'You'll be alright as long as John John is around'. That was his name: John John. So, my other grandfather had the same name as his father and his son and this grandfather was given the same name twice! Perhaps not the most creative way to give someone their name, but it suited them. And same name or not, John John was a man you wouldn't mess with. He always looked like a giant to me because I was so small and he was so tall but he had a very real strength about him, like he wasn't afraid of anything. He is also the man responsible for blessing us all with a wonderful ability to shout and to be heard above all others when needed! When John John gave a direction, people listened and if he shouted I used to imagine wildlife fleeing for cover and people running for shelter for miles around. And yet underneath this big, loud exterior I remember he had the broadest smile and the warmest heart. I used to watch him get ready to go out on some evenings and he was always very dapper. He would have his shoes as shiny as a polished button, and his suit immaculately pressed. My grandfather was a smart man in every sense, and he had a presence that nobody could deny. I called John John 'Dado', and I loved him with all my little heart. When Dado died it was my first major experience of grief and loss. I remember struggling to understand how it could be possible that I would never see him again. I spent a lot of time with my grandmother after he left us, and I will always recall walking upstairs at their house during a sleepover one evening and I felt the familiar brush of my grandfather's hand across my head as I climbed the staircase. I got to the top of the stairs and I could smell him. The arm of a dressing gown was swaying over the banister, which provided the most obvious explanation, but I chose to believe he was right there with me, ruffling my hair with his hand and smiling at me with his big smile. As I have grown up I have felt him around me on many, many occasions, I have felt his strength and his energy. He was such a strong, masculine man I always wondered if he would have understood who I was. As children we don't know who we will become as adults. When society makes your sexuality a big deal you naturally question what loved ones that are no longer around might have thought of you. You almost question the acceptance that you never had the chance to experience because the 'now' you is so different to the 'then' you. Sometimes you allow yourself to think that the person they loved was only part of you, a young, immature part, and so how could you ever be certain they would have accepted the 'full' you, the big picture. I think that answer has to be a simple one: if they loved you then, they would always love you, because in truth, on a spiritual level you are only ever going to be the same soul that they knew. In the real world that sentiment doesn't always cut it, I know. That fear of never knowing acceptance is just another emotional hurdle you face when you become LGBTQ because we are taught that we change, that we make a choice and that choice to many millions in this world is something to still be ashamed of, even murdered for. I don't think personally that choice has anything to do with it, but I am also very passionate about the fact that it shouldn't matter, even if who I am now, is choice. If we decide to be gay, or trans, or to defy the social and cultural ridiculousness of clothes having gender, then good for us. Choice or no choice, it is a decision to live our truth out loud and all we can do is make another decision, and that is to believe that our loved ones who are no longer here, would look upon our truth with love. They would look upon us knowing that the strength we needed to live that truth was partly possible because of the love they brought into our lives.

In summer 2015 I went to see a spiritualist and I was so desperate to have my grandmother come through, but the lady at the reading was very clear that the spirit coming through was who I needed and not necessarily who I wanted in that moment. Who she described could have only been one person. There was no doubt that it was my grandfather, Dado. Before she finished the reading, she said that the spirit knew I was a little different and didn't always know what to make of me, but without any doubt, his love was with me now as strong as it always had been. A few days before the reading I had felt a presence around me, a presence that had in that moment unsettled me in the kitchen of the flat I was living in. She described the feelings I had and the kitchen perfectly, she said that the unsettled feeling of someone stood behind me wasn't fear but an awareness, and it was John John, the smart, tall strong gentleman that would take no messing, the same gentleman that she said would always be with me. That was closure for me, he accepted me after all, how could I have ever allowed myself to think that he wouldn't. I still keep his hat on a table at my house even now, and when I touch it I can see his wonderful smile. The night he died I was afraid to go into his room to see him because I didn't want to see him so poorly and so I stood in the corridor, waiting. On his way out of the room my dad opened the door and I couldn't help but look inside and there he was, smiling that wonderful smile right at me from his hospital bed. I don't think I ever told him that I loved him but I did, and now I'm sure he knows that.

So you see I was blessed with amazing people around me, and as a child I knew unconditional love on a level that was always going to be hard to compete with as an adult. There is no downside to that, but it does bring a realisation as you become an adult that the chances of finding that depth of true, unconditional love in others is an unlikely mission, but a mission filled with expectation created by the immense love you have known. So would I change that? Absolutely not, but do I now have massive expectations of love? Yes, I absolutely do. Expectations that have often left me hurt, confused and disappointed. One thing is certain, and that is that I was taught how to love by being completely and absolutely loved by my family and I will always be aware of how blessed I was to have that.

Madonna & I

School was a blur for me. All those years, all those lessons and all that cruelty. I had two brothers that were much closer to the idea of a 'normal' valleys' boy. My brothers were both older; I was the annoying one that came along when everything was getting settled and peaceful. I always accepted that my brothers were closer to each other because of the age gap and because (let's face it) I was different, different in an odd and confusing kind of way. I don't remember my older brother Geraint much during my childhood because he was ten years older than me so when I was five he was midway through his teens. I do remember him being the rebel, however, a rebel that influenced me to want to go to the opposite extreme, to be good. I would imagine that Geraint has never realised how influential he was, but he was in ways he could never have chosen to be. He was always so angry. I recall endless arguments, screaming and shouting and they usually ended with Mum in floods of tears. I used to stand in the background, silent and terrified. I remember making a vow to myself that I wouldn't be bad. I'd seen bad and because of bad I wanted so desperately to be good. I didn't understand his anger and I loved my parents so much I didn't understand what felt to me like his war against them and the world in general. I have vague memories of a time before that phase of his life and those memories are warmer, funnier, happier. I used to think he must be sad, but I couldn't think of any way to help him. Deep down in my little heart I never believed he could have wanted to be the way he was being, like it must have been a mistake or this crazy person was someone else who just happened to look like my big brother. As the years passed we saw less of the angry teenager until one day he disappeared altogether. But before that angry teenager finally vanished, he left scars and made impressions on me that would be impossible to erase. Aside from teaching me what and who I didn't want to be, he also showed me how terrifying anger could be. He could never have known back then his impact on those around him, especially on the little boy who stood in the corner holding his teddy with tears running down his face, scared to cry out loud in case he was heard. But, in some way those moments made being bullied later in my childhood scarier, not easier. Anger became something to fear because I had seen it in all its grotesque ugliness. I had seen what being the target of anger looked like during and (worse still) after the aggression, and believe me that doesn't prepare you in any way for the terror of one day being the target yourself. Geraint was still my brother and despite all of the times he frightened me and hurt my parents, I still loved him, I never stopped loving him. I was just sorry that we lost him for a while.

I remember Stuart, my other brother, in much more detail; we had to share a bedroom so we couldn't escape each other and the age gap was less, which helped with the bond but still gave him dictatorship in the bedroom sharing arrangement. The bedroom wasn't very big and he had two walls for his posters, which consisted of the rock band KISS and Prince. I was allocated just one small part of a wall, which at the time I decorated with a variety of magazine posters torn from the pages of *Smash Hits*. My wall was small but much prettier than his, and I often used to look at it and think, well age doesn't account for taste.

We had a love-hate relationship. I disliked him deeply in moments and he generally hated me. We had an amazing ability to wind each other up and I blame (or credit) Stuart for some of my finest strop moments and grand, door-slamming exits. In reality I looked up to him and I secretly liked him, and often used to tag along to watch Stuart and his mates breakdance, or to sit on the bed and listen to him playing his guitar. I never wanted to be like him necessarily but I always thought he was clever, cleverer than me, and much to his annoyance I used to like following him about until I crossed the invisible threshold of tolerance! I mentioned before that I was a bit of a talker as a child and so looking back it was to be expected that I frequently got on his nerves. Those talkative moments of mine often prompted from him a variety of overused and understated colourful verbal directions, to which I would respond by declaring my newfound hatred for him before slamming a few doors and retiring back into Christopher-world. One spring I recall that he went on a school trip for a few days to France and I was devastated and outraged all at the same time and I couldn't wait for him to come back. Aside from missing him, the injustice that he should be jetting off while I sulked in my smaller half of our bedroom was more than I could bear! On his return, I had thought that at least I would be compensated for the injustice with a gift. I stared at his suitcase for hours waiting for him to open it. I was sure there had to be something in there for me! Eventually, picking up on my fixation on the very closed case, he agreed to open it instead of opting for torturing me, which would have been so easy. It turned out there was something in there just for me and I was rewarded for my patience with my very first scantily clad muscle man doll! Clearly my brother was a man ahead of his time and he knew his audience very well. It was a He-Man figure. The boy did good.

I remember the day I was offered a promotion at school to a higher class based on my summer exam results. I refused to accept it, afraid of leaving the few friends I had. That night as we were drifting off to sleep Stuart said to me, 'You can't turn down an opportunity like that, you have no idea what one thing could lead to, maybe you're meant to do really well in school, maybe one day you are meant to be prime minister.' I doubt Stuart remembers saying that but the very next day despite my fears I walked straight into the headmaster's office and told him that I had changed my mind. I'm still not prime minister but hey, who knows?

Both of my brothers, along with their various girlfriends that came and went over the years, had to endure my singing and dancing performances. I would make them sit in one armchair at the back of our parents' lounge and I would perform on top of the coffee table. A lot of my parents' furniture had a shiny, high gloss finish to it and my coffee table stage was no different which made it both exciting and terrifying as my dancing feet would glide and spin dangerously in the name of art. I can't decide if those moments form some of their fondest memories or if they are memories they have locked away forever like a trauma. I have a pretty good idea what the answer is, and come to think of it I may have been responsible for a few relationships failing – watching the little brother sing and dance on the coffee table is hardly a girl's idea of a great date. On the other hand, you could argue that I was a useful test. If the girl came back, then maybe she was a keeper? Right? The important thing is that deep down there was always brotherly love and I would do anything for them, I just wish we saw more of each other now we are all grown up. It always felt like the world was a safer place because of the existence of my two older brothers, a feeling I am sure they never realised they had created. Although there are a few exceptions to that sentence. There was that time I told a boy that if he continued to threaten me or carried out said threat to punch me in the face, that my big, scary and brutal older brother would sort him out, and his older brother while he was at it! So there! That feeling was definitely realised by Stuart, who I understand had a few subsequent, challenging chats with the other big brutal older brother! There are also multiple occasions when I have used Geraint's name, in vain during my clubbing days, having thrown diva strops with bouncers on more occasions that he would have liked. I soon realised that bouncers treated me more in the manner I felt I deserved when I mentioned the word 'Flag'. Flag being Geraint's nickname, and with him being a fairly big deal in Welsh security, I found being Flag's little brother a nice little perk in terms of VIP entry and queue avoidance on the Cardiff clubbing scene.

Back in our childhood days, they liked football, rugby and girls. I on the other hand went to dancing, liked cleaning and occasionally flip-flopping about in my mother's heels. My Action Man had a Barbie car, dressing table and a matching wardrobe, need I say anymore? I desperately wanted the Sindy town house for my Action Man to live in, but I think that must have been a step too far for my parents and so he had to slum it in a refurbished crisp box that I decorated with leftover wallpaper, carpet cut-offs and curtain fabric. What's wrong with that? He needed somewhere to put his dressing table and before you ask, no, it wasn't a Walkers Crisps box, it was bigger, stronger and had lining. Anyway, as a child, my pampered Action Man and my passion for dancing, occasional heels, along with my often moody, no-nonsense attitude meant that I was practically walking around the primitively minded valleys of South Wales with a target on my head screaming, 'Come bully me please! I am not like you!'

To add to my proverbial target, I was also so bored with what I saw as the greyness of the rest of the boys in school. They instinctively picked up on two very clear truths, one being that I really didn't fit in to their little boys' club, and secondly, I really didn't want to. I was so internally confused, I sometimes wanted to scream in the middle of the schoolyard, or the street, or even at home to disturb the peace in a tumultuous celebration of otherworldly life. I was captivated by androgyny. I loved watching Prince, Bowie, Grace Jones, Freddie Mercury and Annie Lenox. When I first started seeing these performers on TV I was a child, undamaged by social expectations, and I saw perfectly clearly with no judgement, no label and no inhibitions, I just saw beautiful colourful people who were exactly who I wanted to be when I grew up. I remember seeing Liberace on TV for the first time, he was just spectacular, in a silver diamond- encrusted suit and a feathered cape longer than the entire downstairs of our house! He had more flamboyance than the stage could handle and he looked so happy, so charismatic and so enthralling to watch. His charisma was like electricity and I remember sitting cross-legged as close to the TV as I could get without being told off, just smiling up at the screen in amazement. I remember hearing laughter and derogatory comments coming from behind me. I didn't understand how such beautiful people could be wrong, could be an embarrassment to themselves or something to laugh at. My uncompromised amusement faltered and I remember thinking, maybe I shouldn't like how he looks or how he behaves, maybe I need to laugh at him too. It is so easy to see how the seeds of intolerance are sown and how the unconditioned mind of a child sees no wrong until they are trained to see it. My parents meant no harm, they probably enjoyed it as much as me, but I had begun to understand that the way I saw the world was different to how everyone around me saw it, and I didn't know what it meant for me if I couldn't hide that.

So I was bullied, left out of groups, never picked in sport and was generally an acquired taste. So school from start to finish was interesting. It has to be said that I never really did much to dispel my poor sports reputation. I mean I had perfect coordination and if I could have moved the football around the pitch in the form of a ballroom waltz then I really would have been the next Golden Balls, but in reality my foot and that ball just didn't like each other. My most devastating sporting performance arrived in the form of the annul sports day at school. It was the final relay of the egg and spoon race. My teammates had taken us into the lead and I was the final participant. The crowd started to cheer us all on, the moment arrived and I picked up the spoon and set off. I swear the world went into slow motion, like the scene from *Chariots of Fire*. I could almost hear the suitably dramatic soundtrack. I raced off that starting point like a gold medallist defending their title, and yet my brief promise of glory came to an abrupt end and twisted towards tragedy as in my excited haste my foot caught the back of my other foot and I entered into a prolonged sprawling tumble down the track. I tried desperately to correct myself but I was moving too fast, I zigzagged and dipped like someone having a seizure on a treadmill, ultimately reaching the finish line to a silent, confused crowd and, to the horror of my team mates, with no egg. Needless to say, this was not the start of a triumphant sporting career. It was blatantly clear from that moment that I would never be Golden Balls or Golden Eggs. I pulled myself together and turned to my clearly disappointed teacher and said with all the maturity and dignity I could muster, 'I never liked that stupid egg game anyway, ridiculous that we call it sport. It's an egg on a spoon – it's called breakfast in my house.'

So I was bullied for years, but at the time I am not sure I did feel like a victim, that label, would in itself have been just too much to bear. When I was being bullied I coped with the ridicule and the shame, and locked it all up on the inside, with one primary objective and that was for nobody to see my pain on the outside. I never dwelled on it at school or wanted to make a big deal of it, I really couldn't afford to. I often look back and think about the fact that if I hadn't been bullied then I'm certain my ambition to make something of my life and the thick skin that has protected me along the way may never have developed. However, that is easy to say now from my vantage point as a secure forty-something adult man. How I chose to react to that time in my life was personal to me but any success that I have as an adult will never make the bullying I encountered, okay. I do occasionally think of the younger me and wonder what words of encouragement I would have whispered into the ear of that young, timid boy in the moments he was most afraid. As it turns out, the young Christopher Anstee didn't need those words, but at the time I was terrified and the thing that hurts the most is that most of us have to get through it all alone, which is why some kids don't get through it.

I remember standing outside a classroom waiting for the teacher. The hallway was full of students. I was standing on my own and one of the frequent offenders caught my eye for a split second. That's all it ever took was to catch their eye, then you had to brace yourself for whatever was coming your way. He walked over to me and pushed me against the wall, demanding that I declare that I was 'a queer'. I refused to say it and nudged him back. Within seconds his friends joined in, and the other students in the hallway became spectators. He pushed one hand into my crotch and held it there and used his other hand to push me harder against the wall with his elbow against my shoulder, demanding I say it again, only now he was asking me if I wanted to kiss him. I turned my head away from his face as he released his grip and moved his hands to hold my wrists tight behind my back, forcing his face to mine, laughing a loud, irritating, exaggerated laugh. He was breathing on me and forcing his body so tightly onto mine that I could feel what must have been his erection pushing against my leg. I knew he couldn't do much more because of the students surrounding us but I remember becoming so traumatised that I thought that maybe this is what rape must feel like. I was completely helpless, incapable of pushing him away. In that split second, I was so frightened and I wanted just one person to help me, to stop the humiliation. I could feel tears start to work their way into my eyes but I fought them back with every breath in my body, squeezing my fists so tight at my sides that my nails had started to dig into my skin. Slow motion kicked in as he licked my face. One last hurrah, before returning his hands to my crotch. One person said, 'Just leave it,' without much conviction as they walked away. Everyone else just turned a blind eye and continued with their chitchat. Then it was over, he stood back, placed his hands in his pocket and laughed, turning back to scruff my hair. Almost a gesture of endearment. It staggered me to think that if you give a boy a rep as a hard nut he can molest another boy in front of a crowd and be seen as a crowd pleaser, a comedian or even a momentary hero amongst his crew, and because he is a kid it's okay. It's not okay. I was walking away praying he would ignore me when he pulled me back by my coat hood for some more.

I wanted to cry, more from the shame I felt than anything else, but I looked him right back in the eye as calmly and as slowly as I could. I said only two short words, 'Fuck you.' My grandfather always said if you get into a fight you have to get the first punch in. Perhaps not the most responsible advice, but I knew if I didn't make a swift move it would have got a lot worse, so I dragged my hands free and pushed him as hard as I could and turned to push through the other kids to get away. He caught me of course and persisted in pretending to maul me as I struggled to push him off. Eventually I got away for a second time and ran through the nearest exit and kept going until I got to the school gates. I ran all the way home that day, and had to pretend I had got into a simple fight. As a young teenager you don't want to admit to your parents that you're bullied, it's a sign of weakness and the shame is overpowering at times, especially when you have two older brothers that were so different to you and outwardly so much stronger. Your biggest fear is disappointing someone and admitting that the reason you are being bullied is because every child in the school thinks you're gay, with the exception of a handful of friends. A small handful of friends who also think you're gay I might add, but they are simply being more human and waiting a few years before they ask!

I remember the walk home every night, taking every possible route to avoid certain boys. But it wasn't just boys. It spreads, it spreads like a disease and every person that sees you being bullied gets the green light, the call even, to join in and be the performer. One girl was so cruel that I used to make myself sick worrying about Wednesday afternoons. She sat directly in front of me and took enjoyment in making my life hell not only in those lessons but also on the walk home from school if I was unlucky enough to see her. She never let it rest, she never gave up, spitting, pushing, name-calling, and all because she was convinced I was gay. Well, well done to her. If a gaydar were a GCSE she would have made it to A levels. Unfortunately for her it wasn't.

Unless you've been bullied it's hard to appreciate the sheer magnitude of the panic, helplessness and hopelessness that you feel. You feel weak, a disappointment, a lower level of human being that isn't worthy of escaping your tormentors. There are different classes of kids: bright kids, good-looking kids, sporty kids and funny kids. If you fall somewhere in between those and you aren't any use to anyone, people don't know where to put you and so you become the worst kind of nothing if you let them get away with it. Once it's begun it has the disastrous effect of being self-compounding. You become more and more of a nothing until it feels as though there is little point in your existence. Then, under that growing dark cloud of despair, you have to find the talent to act, act every time you walk through the door at home and pretend that school was good, that you're popular and that you didn't just survive ten rounds of emotional abuse to get through the day. Oh, and on top of that you have to try to concentrate on getting your grades. That was bullying in the 80s, at any rate. I am not sure I would have survived bullying in 2021. It's so, so tough but I knew that I had to take some kind of control. I had to take the control I could take. I'm not particularly brave unless I have to be, but I guess I had to be then. Once I had faced the worst in the scenario and accepted it, for me everything from there got a little bit easier.

So, I kept going back for more. My theory was that if I extinguished the bullies from my mind and acted like I didn't have a care in the world then eventually they would disappear. As Taylor Swift would say, I had to 'Shake It Off' and I did just that. I know this makes it sound easy, and that for some it is so much harder, but as time went on it did get easier. As the months and years passed I turned around my school life. Things that once floored me I would just laugh off. My ability to tear a strip off someone with a sharp comeback improved and sometimes I got the applause and the bully was the one left looking stupid. I had no desire to earn the respect of the people that had been so cruel over the years but in some cases I did just that. I still had the odd 'Anstee, you queer!' or the more regal 'Anstee, you queen!' shouted out during a lesson or across the yard but sometimes I would just laugh because I genuinely found it funny and sometimes they would laugh back with me, as opposed to at me, and then one day, it just stopped.

The one thing that did always piss me off was the fact that they were right, of course. Even though I hadn't even admitted it to myself back then, I was gay and I was a bit of a drama queen, and I probably had the odd diva strop that I failed miserably to hide. I just wish that I had found the courage to embrace it sooner, and I hope with all my heart that as a society we can change so that younger generations can do just that. If we take what makes us different and make it normal then we remove the power from the bully. If we can remove intolerance, then we can empower young human beings to turn around and say, 'Yes I am gay, a queer, a queen. Thank you for taking the time out of your day to remind me of that and a special thank you for your immense powers of observation that frankly the world would struggle to get along without, now you'll have to excuse me while I go to polish my crown.' Better still, they won't even get asked because let's face it: who should care!

In 2021 the world has reached a whole new level of bullying cruelty. It's hard to make my experience relevant against a backdrop of relentless social media that is abused to bring chaos and misery to those targeted. I will never condone bullying; I just can't pretend it got the better of me in the end. I hope that as a society we are helping kids that are different to feel more accepted and by default less different to start with. Unfortunately, the seeds of intolerance that teach the world's innocent minds to hate are all around us. Bullying starts with all of us, we are all responsible for what we say, who we say it to and how we treat each other. If we live with tolerance, then tolerance is what we teach, and even in 2021 the voice of tolerance needs to be desperately louder. We still live in a world where a child with the whole world at their feet can decide to hang themselves from a tree because that is a better option than being who they really are. We live in a progressive world, and even though we like to think we have come a long way, hate is progressing alongside equality, and so we have to keep teaching love so that our kids, nieces, nephews go into schools that make a difficult world a better place to be. At a child's most vulnerable age, one hurtful word can kill. But there is better news, and that is that one kind word can save a life. If you think that is being overly dramatic then you have never experienced the suffocating isolation that bullying can bring. I have felt it, I have seen it and I get it. The good news is that I have also seen it change, I have seen it go away and I have experienced a way of getting through it.

Personal Terrorist

Did you think that I'd forgotten you or the moments when you struck?
With your generous grenades that flew, into my cage, in your perverted zoo
You were my terrorist, I was your sitting duck

I wore your vest of deprivation, while I let you rape me from inside out
You held my power in your detonation, in your twisted circus, your demonstration
In my deafening silence, you heard my shout

Your all or nothing, I was your pick, your tortured soul to bleed and smear
In your grasp a bomb that had started to tick, a frenzied crowd for your tiring trick
In a crown torn from hell, you paraded your queer

In the carnival of fools and fear, an invitation to like and wallow
A refusal to ever shed a tear, to remove the mask through which I'd peer
I emptied my heart in my refusal to follow

In the pits of darkness I saw my hate, my deflection a pity, a weakness you craved
I graced your stage for one final date, a finale to murder my languorous state
By my killing, the end of the freak show I braved

No winner derived any pleasure from pain, the devil in me by the plague that you brought
The blood on your hands still refusing to stain, life's beautiful storm washed it away by the rain
The death of my pain by crucifixion you sought

So did you think you think that I'd forgiven you since I left you at that gate?
With no militia or the me you knew, just a decaying tale that once came true
By my conquering spirit I gave light to your fate

My personal terrorist, the chink in my armour, a childhood destroyer, my stage-stealing stalker
My tale in a bottle still afloat in the sea, my bringer of strength who I keep setting free
Thought I died by your darkness, a revelation saved me

During my time in school I remember briefly thinking maybe I should change to be more like the others. So, despite my better judgment, I gave it a try.

Attempt One: I had decided to join the school football team. I mean, how hard can it be, right? I lasted five minutes before some great big giant of a lad kicked the ball straight into my stunned and somewhat perplexed face. I remember having a full tantrum and marching off the pitch, watched by a small but stunned crowd who at one point I thought might applaud my exit performance. I refrained from turning around to take a bow as I disappeared into the dressing room (I mean changing room). Attempt one officially failed. There was no second attempt; instead I chose Madonna and abnormality.

So, Madonna & I. It's fair to say that it was love at first sight. I was mesmerised by her. I remember singing 'Like a Virgin' repeatedly, feeling naughty every time I got to the chorus. One day I was performing on the staircase, having opened the door to the kitchen so that my parents could hear me, as you do. At first, I said the word 'virgin' quietly and waited for a response. Twenty minutes later I was practically belting it out like Pavarotti while swinging my body around the banisters and across the hallway floor using a white towel to improvise the veil off of the video. It appeared that despite the views of teachers and other kids at that time, in my house the word 'virgin' and Madonna in general were no big deal and more often than not if I was sprawling around on the floor mid performance, I would just be stepped over without interruption like it was all very normal. The result of my experiment was conclusive and a super fan was born. I gratefully accepted my parents' ignorance of my unusual behaviour as acceptance. In that respect I was very blessed. I was able to dance around the house with a T-shirt for a wig, and a blanket for a dress, and as I mentioned earlier, sometimes in a set of heels. I even imitated my mum by running the candy lipstick over my lips before pressing down on some tissue for full effect! Even as a child I was massively aware that clothes had no gender for me, but equally aware that they did for most others. Either way inside my house I could be whoever I wanted to be and I was.

Madonna was the ultimate defiant character. She did what she wanted and she didn't care what people thought about her. It wasn't just about doing things her way, it was about being herself in defiance of the haters and in some obvious way I could identify with that on a much smaller scale. So, Madonna and I danced our way into my teenage years, with a great big raised finger at anyone who had something to say about it. I was only ever going to be me. I was never going to be like my brothers, or conform to my schoolmates' or anyone else's expectations. Conformity was boring and would never be enough to keep me entertained. I wanted more.

So I guess Madonna and I have been through some tough times and managed to get through them together! I was even in the room the night she decided to throw herself off the stage at the Brits, oh the shame! Yes, I know she doesn't know I exist, but thinking, 'What would Madonna do?' got me through a lot when I was a teenager. What can I say; the lady made me human up. I think about Madonna a lot less these days, and thankfully I no longer perform 'Like a Virgin' on random staircases, not because I can't, you understand, just because it isn't really what comes into my head when I'm scaling the staircase on my way out to work in the morning. I do have to be kept away from my V-Limit, however, at all nights out and family parties. My V-Limit is the amount of alcohol I can consume before I get to a fine line between refusing to dance and, a sip of a cocktail later, taking over the whole floor with the whole 'Vogue' routine. I'm not sure I could even remember it sober, but to my absolute horror, once my V-Limit is breached I can recite the whole hand shifting, leg grinding chaos of 'Vogue'. May the random video footage remain hidden forever. Can I get an amen up in here?

So, I will always love her just a little bit for teaching me it was okay to be myself, no matter what anyone else said. When the grown-up world labelled her a whore and a terrible role model for her outspoken views, they failed to see the minority groups of younger people that felt isolated and afraid to admit who they really were.

Madonna was speaking up for the gay community and AIDS education years before Princess Diana made visiting an AIDS ward an acceptable and humanitarian thing to do. The general adult population and parents specifically failed to see that young gay, bisexual, transgender and lesbian kids suddenly had a spokesperson who would teach them to stand up for themselves, to be proud of who they were, to not be afraid and to never compromise their dreams. I am pleased to say that someone growing up today in the west doesn't need that so much, but a lot of people back then did. I did. Being a young gay teenager in the 80s was scary stuff. Not only did we have the fear of being the gay freak that would one day bring shame on the family when we grew up, but we also had to contend with the most awful fear of AIDS as a gay illness.

The Conservative-supported AIDS campaign was so dark and intimidating. I remember that I didn't understand and was too scared to ask anyone about it at first. I was terrified of the TV advertisements, there was an erupting volcano and hands chiselled the words AIDS into a grey tombstone under a darkened sky. The sound of the heavy music haunted the screen and a chilling voice would warn about the spreading disease as the finished tombstone dropped into the dust, along with a spray of lilies. I mean what the hell! That campaign needed a film rating to assess its suitability for certain audiences. It definitely wasn't PG! All I understood was that AIDS was something that gay people got and it was killing thousands all over the world. In the deepest part of my young soul I knew I was gay, so the media effectively served me a death sentence. Every newspaper and every report screamed that this was the gay plague, and if you were gay you were going to get it.

It was a normal school night, and I was just out of my dull uniform and had run down the stairs to bag a good spot at the dinner table. Our house was small and the kitchen table was pushed against the window to create a walkway, leaving just two prime spaces. If you missed one of those spaces, then it was an armchair, lap dinner for you and frankly that wouldn't do! I loved after school time, it was the best time of day for me, and eating was a part of that. The family descended on one disjointed room in the house and there we ate, talked, gave back chat to the TV that was always on in the background, and yes, we sometimes got into good healthy arguments, but it was all real quality together time.

I remember the TV channel being changed to the news and the sinking feeling of seeing the words AIDS behind the presenter as she introduced a victim being interviewed from an unspecified London hospital. I wanted to get up or turn away but I couldn't, I had to watch, maybe they would say something to take this fear away. But it turned out that was wishful thinking. To preserve him and his family and their privacy no name was given, the camera scanned across to the patient's bed and he was lying there, the bedclothes hung loosely around the bottom half of his body. You could barely see any rise in the bed covers where his legs should have been and his torso had been cruelly ravaged to the point where he was just emaciated, there were just bones, and dark lesions all over his chest and face and his teeth had become pronounced as the skin around his skull was tight, almost transparent. I wanted to cry. I felt my heart bouncing inside my chest and I started to feel panicked. Everyone else in the room was continuing to eat as normal, but I was scared that my emerging panic and fear was visible. The man on the TV was so young, I remember he had beautiful eyes and was smiling. How could he be smiling? how could he even speak through the decaying state of his life and body? This life that was clearly still hanging on to threads of hope was smiling and here I was terrified, frozen. After the short interview the clip cut back to the news studio where the presenter confirmed that the man had died since the interview was recorded. I was engulfed with pity, fear and sorrow. I was going to cry, I couldn't stop it. I got off my chair and ran from the room, out of the kitchen and straight up the stairs and into the bathroom, the only place where I could be locked safely away. Within seconds my mum had hurried after me and shouted from the foot of the stairs. I faked an upset tummy, which gave me ten more minutes of space to breathe. I was just a child, but I was in solution mode as I sat hugging my knees on the floor of the bathroom with my back against the door. I told myself that it was okay, I needed to make sure I was straight, whatever that meant, and if I couldn't do that then I needed get through school and then run away, and then in my irrational young mind I decided that my final fall back if everything else failed was that I would just kill myself the minute I got AIDS. Then silence. Then the tears stopped. It was okay because I had a plan. The feelings that replaced my ebbing panic that night were emotions of loss. I almost mourned the life of that tragic but beautiful man on the TV. I didn't eat that night, I couldn't, and so the tummy upset story worked out well. I went to bed early without being asked and blocked out the world.

As the weeks passed I would continue to feel the fear of seeing headlines land on our doormat, but my fear broke into a desperate desire to understand. Instead of running from it, I actively started looking for information. Over a period of years, I learned a lot, I started to grow up, to gather perspective and my eyes began to open much wider than the hate, intolerance and injustice that was being served by governments around the world. Leaders were turning a blind eye to the pain and suffering of one community that frankly most governments wanted to just disappear. Their blood-soaked hands and belief systems were getting their wish!

Before the AIDS epidemic, New York, like other western cities, had become a shining beacon. They became the emerald cities of gay life. New York, San Francisco, LA, London all became figurative LGBT refugee camps as the young men and women gravitated down the often broken and twisted yellow brick roads that lead them out of the suffocating intolerance and ignorance of their small hometowns. Under the bright lights of the city, communities began to thrive as they became absorbed into the rich, bustling tapestry of art and culture. I guess you could say that in this Oz the wizard was freedom, freedom to be whoever the hell you wanted to be. I was too young to experience that and too late to appreciate how it felt when I eventually did get to New York, but as a young gay adult who had grown up as a spectator of what I thought was the bold and the beautiful US of A, I was hungry to learn more. Wasn't it the wonderful Maya Angelou who said, 'The more you know of your history, the more liberated you are.' I read, watched and absorbed as much about the New York LGBT community as I could, and what I got, in mere bursts and snapshots, was a glimpse of the rich energy that was created by those dazzling young spirits who blazed a trail for the rest of us. It is said that Christopher Street, which is 9th Street, west of 6th Avenue in Manhattan, was spectacular in its heyday. The atmosphere full of carnival-like electricity, as people found freedom in the moment to express themselves, with vivacious style, boldness and power. The streets bustled with the eclectic flamboyance of lives being lived by those once caged. The streets would become catwalks not of beauty but of pride, where these young, often abused and dismissed human beings, grew confident, grew loud and grew in purpose. On those streets, like many others across the world, in the safety of a growing numbers, people found a place to belong, to grow strong and to develop a perspective that reminded them that life wasn't always fair or equal or just, and it showed them that they had the power to change it.

AIDS stripped the colour from the once rainbow-spirited streets of Greenwich Village and left dramatic scars on the community. In 1981, AIDS was thought to be a new and rare form of cancer that only gay men developed. Nobody stopped the party at first, but within two years hospitals were overrun, people were being fired for just being gay or even associated with the gay community. Hate and intolerance started to rear its ugly head and the world became crippled with fear. Gay men both well and unwell were becoming homeless and destitute. If that wasn't enough, mistreatment and abandonment followed these young men and in some but fewer cases, young women to their graves. Hospitals had whole floors sectioned off as limited staff with often little nursing experience worked head to toe in PPE for long hours in hideous conditions. The patients had no TVs as the technicians who were required to get them working in those days refused to enter their rooms. They had few visitors and as the months passed an increasing number of patients had already watched their partners and closest friends die. They had already witnessed the pain that was to be their own fate. Food was often cold and inedible as catering staff would only be prepared to push trollies out of the lift onto the floors for the already-stretched nurses to serve. Due to the lack of investment and the persistent, wilful ignorance of the government, some of the early treatments were slow to appear and when they did surface, they brought more pain and suffering than the illness itself. Soon many hospitals reached breaking point and the sheer volume of those dying had to be taken care of. These were often young people who had escaped violence or abuse to make a life for themselves far away from what they had once called home. What made the situation so heartbreaking was that thousands of beautiful souls had sadly severed connections with family who had thrown them out and cut them off. Suddenly these newly orphaned human beings belonged to nobody that could afford to bury them. In their hundreds the dead were taken in cardboard boxes on trucks once a week to mass graves in Potters Field, Heart Island where they were left in unmarked graves. I can't decide what must have been worse, the fear and loss caused by the pandemic itself or the knowledge that overwhelming portions of society, with the help of the media, not only turned a blind eye, but they did so with disgust. Disgust and hope that this disease-ridden community would soon all be gone or reduced enough to be placed in a neat little box where they could be unheard, unseen and controlled.

Thousands died of AIDS; in New York alone 100,000 people have lost their fight with the disease, and a massive 10,000 in the UK. From the liberation days of Stonewall and the spectacular progress of the activists who rose in the 60s and 70s like the wonderful Marsha P. Johnson, Sylvia Rivera and Harvey Milk, the 80s brought a battle that not only wiped out thousands of the LGBT community but also an illness that cruelly set back the equality movement by at least twenty years.

All of that was going on while I sat, terrified, on my parents' bathroom floor. I was frightened of what I might become, ignorant to the pain, suffering and fight that these spectacular communities were living through. A community I was soon to realise was my community, my brothers, my sisters and my people. It's hard to read, watch or study our history without being overwhelmed with pure heartfelt PRIDE and an absolute sense that you are and always will be part of the most spectacular family.

The only thing that terrifies me now is the thought of being anything else other than who I am, an ecstatically proud gay man, but that took some time to get to and there was no sugar coating the fear faced by young gay men and women growing up in the 80s. The only good thing I can take from growing up in that era was that in some ways the fear of that campaign stayed with me into my adult life and became part of my consciousness; it gave me enough fear to ensure that I would always look after myself. The AIDS campaign was hailed as a success, and it may well have been, but it also helped turn gay people into lepers in the mind of society and initiated a swell of gay intolerance; suddenly if you were gay, it was only a matter of time before you had the disease. The slogan was 'Don't Die of Ignorance', and yet that is exactly what the campaign created. For years many parents would need to call help lines when their children came out because they were convinced that just by being gay, their child would at some point become HIV positive. You might read that and think, really? Come on! But the sad truth is that mindset was created, it did exist. My own mother feared the very same thing, and my brother had to take leaflets on HIV to her so that she would start to understand that gay didn't equal AIDS. My brother had to educate my mother to accept the truth. It wasn't her fault and it was her love and worry for me that triggered the thought process that had been planted, not just in my mam's mind but the minds of millions. I often wonder how much easier it would have been for gay people if that stigma had never existed. So the campaign did do what it intended to do but without the concurrent support and education required to create a tolerant society, and so a very real stigma was used and escalated, to the detriment of a community already struggling to find equality. Maybe in 2021 the world has gone too far in the opposite direction and maybe the blind eye that government and society now appear to be taking towards HIV is just as irresponsible. Time will tell, but instead of preventing STIs, the world appears to have settled into the notion that it's okay because now we can just spend millions on treating them or preventing them instead.

If we were all really honest, the stigma of HIV and AIDS is still very much associated with gay men, but thankfully gay men are no longer defined by it. A new time had arrived and as we hit the 90s having a gay friend or relative had started to become less of a dark secret and more of a fashion accessory, still a novelty of sorts but absolutely more of a celebratory thing. Gay men were no longer pushed into the shadows but were now being paraded and in many ways celebrated by the world. In 2021 I would like to think that having a gay friend simply means that you have a friend, no novelty, no big deal and no show pony. Having said that, gay people don't aspire to just be like everyone else anymore. The struggle for equality has made the gay community want much more than that. The LGBTQ communities that I have come to know now want to stand out from the crowd for real and justified reasons. We want to be proud of the men and women who fought to overcome hate in earlier generations and we want to be celebrated for exactly who we are, not just allowed to join in straight people's version of what seems like a good life. Some people will say that it should be just about being equal and, in many respects, it is, but when you have been a minority that's been through many struggles to get to that equality, suddenly you have a heritage and a history that you want to hold onto, a history that does make you proudly different and a strength of identity that is worth protecting. On top of all of that, there is still so much to be done, so many to help, and so many more barriers to cross. We are evolved but nowhere near where we need to be. Occasionally as a gay adult I get asked, why do you guys still need Pride!? I never dignify that question with a full answer, but suggest that somewhere in the ignorance of the questions, lies the answer.

So finally, my Madonna point? Well, the point is that Madonna was my Marsha P. Johnson and my Harvey Milk. She did not only change the world, she showed us how to do it, and she extended an invitation for the world to do it for themselves. Not by demonstrating on the streets but in demonstrating through her music, her performance and with her voice. She invited us to stand up, to embrace our own voice, not in terms of world politics or the rights and wrongs of society, but more importantly about who we are and being who we are no matter what courage that takes. It probably sounds silly, but to a young gay teenager she appeared fearless and she did more than just make me stand up for who I was, she made me want to be that person with pride. Madonna was the person who finally made me see that proving my bullies right was my power, being my truest self out loud was my power, saying 'so what' was my power and refusing to back down on who I was, was my power and my story. If the world wanted to call me a Queen for becoming a proud queer, then okay. No man, woman or bully was going to rain on my parade, but as for me, well I was determined to reign all over it!

Miss M & I

I have a little tale to tell about a Lady who taught me well
Who gave me fuel to start my fire
Who helped me kill the secret liar
Who put the rainbow in my hand, who invited me to take the stand
Invited me to smash survival, to gun down doors to my arrival

I had to learn to live not hide, to love myself to feel the pride
To win the war with words not fight
To break the barricade with light
I tore down walls of phoniness and swept away life's loneliness
I tore apart the angry cage, that housed my hungry heart of rage

I had to grow into the man, to show the world just what I am
To lead my destiny by choice
To lift my head and use my voice
Her shadow always on my ground, but I walked my way, I made my sound
The Lady taught me not to wait, to trample fear, to become the great

Into my world I stand alone, forearmed with wisdom I was shown
Ambition that is truly mine
To conquer life to seize my time
From afar she changed my heart, but on the earth we walk apart
So take a look behind my eyes and there you'll find Miss M & I

Narnia

As it turns out, at the age of sixteen I was still alive. Not yet hung out to dry or marched out of the small, sleepy town that I called home. I had developed an actual interest in watching rugby and even had a hand holding, kissy cuddly-style girlfriend called Charlotte. I was hitting the confused years! Charlotte was a dancing, wannabe actress and I was the next big singer songwriter who was going to illuminate the music scene, like a big, beautiful firework that would capture the hearts of the millions. I wrote songs – I wrote lots of songs, in fact it's all I did for months. Locked away in what was still only my half of my little valleys' bedroom, I taught myself how to play basic chords on the piano, just enough to enable me to write my own songs. There was no You Tube back then, just books, lots and lots of big heavy and sometimes smelly books that I had to painstakingly carry back and forth to the library in town. I wasn't lazy as such, but let's just say that my arms were small and the hills and books were big! I was painfully slow to start but I got better, and even though the budget would only stretch to a basic Casio keyboard, it was enough to get me going. In my little world behind that bedroom door, there were moments when that keyboard could have been the finest Bösendorfer, and I the young Elton John whipping up my crowd, sweat running down my face and onto my sequined lapels as the heat of a thousand stage lights flashed all around me. The reality, I am sure you will appreciate, was much more stripped back than that. In fact, I was never really a sweater, thank the lord, and my lighting was a wonky red clip lamp that had lost its arm strength, therefore needing copious amounts of encouragement to stay up while I clumsily navigated across the Casio keys! However, there were definitely sequins. One night as I stared out of my lonely bedroom window I saw thousands and thousands of stars lighting up the sky. They reminded me of tiny sequins all sewn into the fabric of the mystical night sky. Sequins, I thought, now wouldn't that be a blast! A few short moments later I had tiptoed across the landing and into my parents' room, where I proceeded to gingerly open my mam's wardrobe. I knew for a fact that there were more than a few sequins and shoulder pads in that closet. Don't judge, it was the early 90s and most women had kept a few of their 80s fashion pieces, almost like a fashion hangover if you will, and there it was, the one! Yes, okay, it was officially a blouse, but sprinkle that garment with some imagination and you had a rock star costume. I tried it on and made myself laugh as I gazed into the mirror, pulling shapes and faces that my mother had pulled a thousand times as I watched and waited outside ladies' changing rooms. There was no time for a movie montage, however, and not wanting to be greedy I grabbed the one and closed the closet. Adorned in my new costume I then had the even more dangerous task of getting back across the landing and into my bedroom. As I stood in the doorway it felt like such a risky journey, almost requiring a Bear Grylls-style tactical plan. I took a deep breath and bounced across that two and a half meters of landing and threw myself into my room. If the walls had eyes that night I probably would have looked like a heavily emblazoned clutch bag being thrown across a small room, but hey, I made it back, I was safe!

It was a purple number that rested slightly open at the front, and dazzled as I moved under the wonky red lamp. It made me feel all Bowie-esque, rockstar-ish and rebellious. The truth is that I probably just looked like a very tasteless and badly dressed teenager. I wanted to be Ziggy Stardust but probably looked more like Dick Emery without the wig! My audience, however, was epic, and nobody could take that away from me. Prince, Paul Stanley, Gene Simmons, Madonna, Jackson, Whitney and Barbra all watched over me from those bedroom walls – what a treat that must have been for them. You think?

I was bitten by the bug. I couldn't stop writing. I played, I paced, I dressed up, I played, I wrote, I paced some more and sometimes in the end I created something not half bad. I remember my brother Stuart, who was already a spectacular guitar player, being my biggest critic. He would try to explain how to learn faster and how to get clever but I hated being told anything. I was impatient and moody and wanted to learn for myself. I remember one day I played a new song called 'Boulevard' and instead of stopping me and telling me what to change, he listened to the whole thing. When I finished, he said, 'That's not bad you know,' and I knew that small compliment must have meant it was even a bit better than that.

Around that time I had seen Whitney Houston perform in London and soon after I had experienced my first live Michael Jackson concert at a sold-out show at the Cardiff Stadium. I was mesmerised by them both, almost obsessed not only with the power of their sound but the power they had to lift thousands of people into a frenzy. They were life-altering shows for me. But more than the power of the music I was captivated by the theatre of the shows: the lights, the staging, and most of all the eloquence of the dancers. I was desperate to pack my bags and run with my keyboard and books to the nearest dance school, I wanted that to be me up there on that stage mesmerising the crowd. I didn't necessarily want to be Whitney or Jackson, but I did want to be a dancer. So that was it, I would carry on writing but as a side line I would dance my way onto the world stage. Maybe Madonna was touring soon, maybe she needed a little Anstee in a sequined blouse to bust some moves for her? Such an easy plan, what could possibly go wrong, right?

Like me, Charlotte had creative, diva tendencies and was also going to be an award-winning performer. So in that respect at least we were a good match. But sadly, despite the long golden locks and the hand holding moments of romance at a spectacular Take That concert, Charlotte and I never made it. You see, the cruel truth was that I loved another. A cold, one-sided forbidden love but love nonetheless. I was sixteen and I had fallen in love for the first time. It was never going to work for many reasons, the main reason being I had fallen in love with Mark Owen from Take That. I remember actually thinking at the time that the commute to Manchester in itself was a hike and long-distance celebrity relationships never seemed to last. But give me a break, I was a teenager! Oh, and then there was the other. Not so new but now much more absolute revelation – I liked men more than women!

Charlotte wasn't my only girlfriend but let's be real here, there wasn't a long line. Charlotte was someone I thought I genuinely loved at one stage. I cared for her and I thought she was beautiful, witty, dramatic and funny. She made me laugh and she made me feel wanted even though we were just kids. In a fleeting moment I almost didn't want to be gay, I wanted to be normal (whatever the hell that was), What made it even more convincing is that I actually felt the attraction. It wasn't all smoke and mirrors, I did want to be with Charlotte, I remember that very clearly. A few boys in our year at school felt the same and I guess that made me feel like the lucky one, but I knew I liked men more, much more. At that age we feel like we can conquer the world, so God forbid we should feel held back or restricted but I knew I wasn't living the truth I believed in so much. Part of me had developed an aggravation towards society's demands on labelling me and I wanted to resist it. Charlotte wasn't part of that fight and I wasn't ashamed of finding men attractive, but I thought that it was a restrictive state, a statement of limits that defined me and labelled me only to help others put me in a box. I am not sure how long I struggled with that concept, but I started to realise that I was missing something, I was missing a vital piece of a very unfinished jigsaw and that was the connection with owning who I was for the good of standing up to hate and intolerance. If I wasn't going to formally label myself, how could I be myself with pride and stand up for what would become my community, and how was I going to look at bullies straight in the eye and say, 'so what, yes I am gay and that is okay.' If I am honest I guess I still struggle with being defined in any specific way and that has nothing to do with the lifestyle I lead or the choices I make, I am proud of them all, I am just hoping for a future where we don't have to be known by anything other than equal human beings. I sometimes have to really ponder on the purpose and needs of the many, many boxes that now line the shelves of human categorisation and sometimes I think we should take a match to all of them, but not yet! Despite much procrastination I always arrive at the same conclusion and that is, that right now we need the labels that allow us to fight intolerance, to self-identify, to express ourselves in whatever way we want to. How we identify also helps us to educate the world that different is okay, different is good, acceptance of difference is the beginning of the end of inequality. It helps us focus on the fact that equality is everyone's business and no human being or group is exempt. More importantly than all of that, right now communities founded on identity, help us find family, a sense of belonging and a way to show the world that we are proud of who we really are, in our truth.

So ultimately, I stripped back the wrappers of confusion and teenage aggression and found my peace with who I was and how I wanted to identify. I opened that proverbial box labelled gay, the box I imagined to be covered in glitter beneath a shimmering shroud of fairy dust and I jumped in head first. After all, if you were going to choose a box why the hell chose anything other than that one. Right?

My best friend then and to this day was Rhoda. Rhoda (aka Jonathan

Bradley Tarr) was my friend, comedy partner and brother from another mother for the best part of my early life. We were the real rebels. When others were out taking drugs, smoking and drinking as much alcohol as possible, Jonathan and I were at my house giving each other scores out of ten for lip syncing to records and wearing T-shirts on our heads in a bid to experience long rock star hair. I say rock star, I think we both knew we both wanted to be more Mariah than Metallica! When we got bored of that we would usually learn and recite whole scenes from French & Saunders, and on occasion we would give our mates a run through, which sounds horrific but usually brought the house down. 'Don't feed the stars, Dott! I bet he does tricks!' (If you watched it, you'll get it, and if you didn't, you really should.)

Jonathan was and now will always be the only person that has shared every single emotion I have been through in my life. We grew up together. We literally were very rarely apart with the exception of the odd holiday, but we even went on most of them together. The one time I didn't go, Jonathan returned seven days later dressed in cycling shorts and sporting a rather large bum bag! I opened the door to my house and he just stood there. 'So, what do you think?' I am not sure if I ever found the right words, but it was proof enough that he couldn't be trusted to go shopping without his best amigo. We built Lego, we played with cars, we became teenagers and 'pretended' to lust after girls, we discovered music and fashion, we argued, we made up, we watched TV, we learned how to drive and more importantly than anything else we made each other laugh, all the time. Jonathan even taught me how to drive until the day I forgot how to stop and drove straight over a roundabout!

In a nutshell, Rhoda is one of life's good guys and I was lucky to have him as my best friend. Anyway, as it turns out, Jonathan (or Rhoda as I fondly call him) was also gay and was in love with Jason Orange, also from Take That, so double dating could have so worked! We never really admitted that to each other at the time, but we secretly knew, and one day over a glass of sangria or twenty I spilt the beans. But before I tell you all about that I should probably explain, 'why Rhoda?'

There is a car scene in the spectacular classic *Romy and Michelle's High School Reunion* that defines our friendship, and from first watch and from that day forward we vowed that we would be known as the Mary and/or the Rhoda, and unfortunately, we will spend the rest of our lives disagreeing on who is who, but this is my book and so right here on this page, I am definitely the Mary!

It was obvious to me that if I ever was going to come out it would be to Jonathan, but alas on that special night as the clock struck midnight, Rhoda was very drunk, rolling around on the beach from an excessive sangria intake. So under the light of the moon, in the throes of one of our many deep and meaningful discussions, I shared my news with my other best buddy, the one and only Sazzle Evans. Sazzle, the friend formally known as Sarah Evans, always had the ability to make me talk. Not that talking was ever an issue for me, in fact the problem is that I often find it difficult to stop, but Sazzle had a way of getting the deep stuff out, and she still does.

Sazzle is the kind of friend that would drop her life and travel to the moon and back to help you if she could. Sazzle was gifted with the ability to press all of my good (and some of my bad) buttons, but most importantly Sazzle and Rhoda are at sibling status. An argument or a row wouldn't be enough to break our friendship; it runs far too deep. We are stuck with each other for better or for worse, probably better for me and worse for them, but we are stuck together nonetheless.

So let me paint the scene. I was now eighteen and Rhoda, Sazzle and I had embarked on our first 18 to 30s trip. It was a warm Ibiza night, five jugs of sangria had been consumed and a sixth had been ordered, while insulting the barman by trying to speak Spanish very badly. If my memory serves me correctly Sazzle asked for 'Uno plaino packeto de crispo' very proudly but probably incomprehensibly due to the fact that by that point we were both made up of forty per cent red wine and fruit. You know the effort is futile when you then have to repeat the request in an emphasised Queen's English to get the crisps.

There was cheap porn film-style Spanish music playing from the terrace and the sea was softly caressing the shore and thankfully not taking Rhoda with it as it receded. It was still so warm and the sky was a dark clear blue and the lights from across the bay sparkled on the dark water. We were sat outside on the spot that has since become the Café Del Mar, but there were no drugs or flamethrowers or generally very cool DJs on this night. On this night there was me, Sazzle, Rhoda pretending to be a seal, and a barman who clearly would have preferred to be anywhere else but was smiling through it anyway. I had just finished telling Sazzle about an encounter with a 'man', and now, there was a moment of silence.

I had done it: I was out. At that moment I was expecting fireworks and Diana Ross to raise up out of the floor in sequins with a full backing troop singing, 'I'm Coming Out', followed by Gloria Gaynor and finally Judy Garland performing a dance version of 'Over the Rainbow' on a crystal unicorn for the ultimate grand finale. It is fair to say that the line-up would have changed had it been today, but equally fair to say that the original line-up was not without fault, given that Judy was already dead. Anyway, in reality, all I could hear was the slurp and slop of Sazzle taking another gulp of sangria while trying to steady her drinking elbow on the table before letting out a short burp. Rhoda was now singing 'Circle In the Sand' by Belinda Carlisle, while still rolling around in the actual sand somewhere in the distance. My initial fears were confirmed. The story about the encounter had failed, and the bit about the encounter being with a man specifically had failed to register and I was still officially straight! It took a whole new night and a further substantial investment in sangria and Belinda Carlisle before we got there. Sometimes you just have to say it, and so I did… kind of! I don't know what happened, but just as the words 'I'm gay' were about to leave my mouth a translation occurred and I heard myself saying, 'I'm bisexual'! Not as dramatic at all, and the look on their faces was one of bemusement and not of shock. But even if I only had a leg and an arm and half my head out of the closet, at least I had waved goodbye to Narnia. I was bisexual with the full intention of promoting myself to gay in the next six months. It was like that moment when you approach a buffet table with the intention of eating a small salad and leave with two plates full of pastries, pretending you have a hungry friend with a broken leg back at your table. The intention was there. But hey, one buffet plate at a time, as they say.

The following four years became about friends, work and travel. I had always been comfortable with who I was but wasn't yet ready to tell my folks or my brothers. I would when I was good and ready.

The other reason was that while I was brilliant at being gay in terms of my passion for fashion, my musical heroes and the odd diva-style 'my way or the highway' moment, I was really quite poor at doing anything about it in terms of meeting someone. That wasn't what my life was about back then. I had everything I wanted and I can't remember wanting a boyfriend. After all, by that time I had worked through a series of 'would be, should be' famous boyfriends. I had found and lost love with Mark Owen, Matthew McConaughey, Keanu Reeves and an Italian singer called Eros Ramazzotti. I was exhausted!

I had partied in London, Vegas, stood on the edge of the Grand Canyon, walked amongst the Pyramids, performed in Ayia Napa with my lovely singing mate Hayley Alexander-Luff and returned back to Ibiza for old times' sake. I had auditioned for the Welsh National Opera, completed youth opera workshops, started and finished a band called Rezonate, auditioned for a boy band called 'Justin' and got down to the final ten, become a roller blading genius and retired my dancing dream with the exception of podium dancing in nightclubs. Nightclub dancing was there to stay. Once I had a beer in my hand and had caught sight of a podium, I was off, clambering my way to the top with not-very-subtle dance moves, ejecting my competitors from the platform with my posterior to secure my place. Michelle (aka Michael), Rhoda and Sazzle would watch with their hands over their eyes, amazed that once again I had avoided being punched in the face. I couldn't help it and I loved it. There is no feeling like dancing your heart out to the beat of euphoric music amongst a crowd of hundreds. I forget the number of nights we all walked home across London in the daylight, high. Not on drugs but purely on life. Happy days.

In the beginning there was fear, there was trepidation and a sense of overwhelming caution, but those things passed away and were replaced with pure unadulterated life! When my friends and I first hit the gay night scene, we literally had no expectations but we did feel rebellious for walking through the doors of the venue. Back in the early 90s there was still the remnants of very real street homophobia, and it was common to be remarked upon for stepping in and out of certain bars or clubs. We used to let that intimidate us, I even had friends who would give a different, nearby venue name to cab drivers to avoid the stigma. That didn't last long and before you knew it Saturday night became the only time in the week that mattered. We started to find our identity, our community and our place on the dancefloor. Not just one but every venue across the city. We drank and flirted and pranced and danced all over Cardiff, often half a bottle of vodka down before even getting in the cab to hit town. The ambiance would start the minute you sashayed into a friend's place to get ready, often turning the pad into a giant dressing room that would also become a catwalk, cocktail bar and dance floor! We were unstoppable, and no slur or remark on the street was ever going to stop us once we had found our groove, in fact we eventually welcomed the attention, because then we felt proud, defiant and powerful! The excitement and the anticipation consumed the energy during each minibus cab ride into town, in fact I am surprised the drivers could hear themselves speak, often being directed by us to crank up the tunes and adjust the station. We would all be wearing something newly purchased that day, pushing the boundaries of mainstream to gay fashion, some more than others. I used to spend so much money on getting my hair styled, I must have been crazy, I mean there wasn't much of it! I wasn't satisfied with just anyone you understand, oh no, I needed creative flair! And so would only use the style director at Toni & Guy on St Marys Street. I forget her name, but she was flawless and cutting edge, well that's what I thought and that's exactly what I was hoping she would muster up on my head. The trouble with me was that I thought I was Madonna but had the budget of a teenager with an average size paper round!!!! It turns out being a good gay was expensive! So, I went through the colour charts more than a few times, sometimes red, sometimes blond, sometimes streaks of white, and just the once a Mohawk style do that had purple tips that were three shades brighter than I had hoped. So new clothes and hair was a big deal, but then there was the make up! Most of us wore it but mostly only just enough to detect a subtle glow. It felt brave to walk out of the door with eyeliner, bronzer and a clear lip gloss on! If you were a goth, David Bowie or Boy George, you could wear make-up and be awarded the cool goth or general legend badge. If you were just gay and colourful, no such awards were offered up. Instead, it was just another reason to attract the wrong kind of attention, or for people to draw the wrong stereotypical conclusions! I for one never let that stop me, I did it all, lip gloss, eye liner, bronzer, nail varnish and if I was really going for it, I'd find room for glitter spray! If I was going out, out I was getting Kyliefied! When I look back, I can see how brilliant we all were. Not because of how we may have looked, but because of how we felt; we were all such a force, a hedonistic tribe who just longed to laugh, dance and parade about with our own people where we felt safe and where we felt authentically us. The thrill of the first step into the club was electric. Lights dazzling, music pumping and the smell of perfume and aftershave all combined to create an orgy of the senses. Without fail, and before we would push open the doors of the club, one of us would always remember to deliver our mantra, 'Now remember girls, we're pop stars.'

Those big nights out always ended in the same way, with dancing into the very early hours! It was always the ultimate feel-good release, the trip that elevated your mind and body out of the day-to-day noise and chaos and into somewhere otherwise unreachable! That wasn't new for me, but had become my way of experiencing it.

Every kid has a dream, and my big dream was to dance. I felt energy for it, like it was in my blood. When I danced, even at the youngest age, I felt like I was connected to something else, something greater than me, an almost vehement force. I would go to dance classes and watch every foot movement and listen to every instruction, blocking out the noise of the meaningless chit chat from the other kids that served only to annoy me; I wanted the teacher all to myself. At a young age I had developed the ability to be en pointe without a pointe shoe in sight. The technical ability to hold your whole-body weight on the tips of your fully extended toes gives the dancer such grace and a weightless, sylph-like appearance, and the pain of doing it raw without the shoes was an addictive, intense pain. It felt like the pain was giving my body strength and energy and so I gave into it time after time, dancing my way through it in any space I could find. I would walk and spin and show off my en pointe whenever I could, blissfully unaware of the damage I was doing without the proper shoe structure. But had I had those shoes, then what I was doing wouldn't have felt special, and so behind closed doors I continued to practice, over and over again.

I used to sit watching dancers on the TV, jealous that they were up there doing it, not pretending like me but actually doing it. As I got older I still gravitated towards the dancers in a show, sometimes paying more attention to them than the headline act. I wanted to be like Randy Allaire and Salim (a.k.a. 'Slam') Gauwloos. They were not just amazing dancers who had made it to the top of their game, they were special, they were different, and they oozed attitude and spirit that captivated me and transcended my expectations of a human being that could dance. In performance they were more than just dancers, they were dazzling and very beautiful.

I don't know for sure what happened. I guess maybe the dream wasn't big enough or I wasn't disciplined enough, but one way or another, life happened and I let it all go. I got side tracked and I allowed life to get in the way, I confused myself with who I was and what I wanted and let society kill that part of me that was once so sure. I let bullies trigger a thought process that made me feel weak, and yet the weakness was not in the dancing itself, but the inner saboteur that I allowed to speak. I was the one responsible for my dreams and I let myself down, nobody else. It was me that let the world in, and I let the world interfere with what I wanted to be. Maybe my inner demons were more powerful than any of my tangible enemies. Come to think of it, they probably still are.

The Mellifluous Dancer

I am the dancer
In my blood he will dwell
A mesmerised soul
A fairy-tale spell

Expressionist truth
Ephemeral light
Incipient ambition
Eloquent flight

A wish to be taken
A surrender to sound
Shape-shifting beauty
Divorcing the ground

Graceful with brawn
Exquisite the trance
Twisting my aura
Prepossessing romance

Delicate magic
The soaring serene
A menacing torso
Possessed by the dream

A vulnerable spirit
So fragile in form
Embracing the passion
To ever perform

Eyes in the darkness
Watching his pray
The mellifluous dancer
Sings in sauté

The real black Swan
Killing my lust
Ebullience drowning
In the lake full of dust

Magnificent force
Suppressing my lilt
The reeds where I hide
Beginning to wilt

Under the moonlight
A sumptuous end
My epiphany served
The feathers descend

Lifted and lifeless
I give into his heart
His tears to my death
Let the symphony start

Ambitions & Bath Taps

Having had a number of creative ideas expire, I announced that I was going to be a painter. I mean for goodness' sake, there must be something I was spectacular at, right? I had pictured myself walking around with my latest portfolio under my arm, and grand openings of my work in the world's finest galleries. I would be a bohemian of means, of course, and live in Montmartre, Paris in a rooftop flat with views of the Sacré-Coeur. I would dine in the finest restaurants and travel by private jet all over the world to fulfil lavish commissions.

Back in the reality of the Welsh Valleys it was Christmas morning, and I awoke to the oils, the easel, professional brushes and all of the creative ambition I needed to paint my first masterpiece. I was set. Christmas and New Year passed, and I waited until January to start my work. I picked my subject. I decided on a realist landscape oil painting that would incorporate my parents' house, the part of the world I was most familiar with. I laid out all the materials and put on some soothing music to create the perfect mood. I dressed in a loose-fitting white top and had a supply of fresh water at the side of the easel to keep me refreshed and alert to the needs of my creative flow. The moment had arrived, and with a deep breath I lifted the brush. There is no other way to describe my painting; it was a great big pile of sh – disaster. Worst of all, I discovered that I was a rubbish painter. Realism is the precise, detailed and accurate representation in art of the visual appearance of scenes and objects. My painting, however, was the most imprecise and inaccurate drawing I have ever seen. In fact, it was so bad I tried to blur the colours to create something a bit more abstract. Unfortunately, in the process all I managed to create was a mess that looked like someone had failed to paint something beautiful and instead had rubbed everything together in a failed attempt at creating something abstract. Funny that! In under an hour my painting career had started, finished and the materials had been placed neatly in the back of my wardrobe. The tickets to Paris were cancelled. I'm not sure I was ever cut out for a life of Parisian frivolity anyway. Cardiff was much prettier.

Did I give in too easily? Probably. But there was no love in that brush and there was certainly no talent on that canvas. I may be a

Libran and I may struggle on those big old decision scales when I can't decide, but I am brilliant at knowing my certainties and I really didn't like painting. This Picasso had packed up and packed in.

I had started to write short stories around that time, but I threw them all away one by one. I had started to pick the keyboard back up and had written somewhere in the region of one hundred new songs and then in between all of that, had short blasts of trying to write poetry.

One night, I recall having an incredibly vivid dream. I was in my parents' house and I was awoken from my sleep by a notion to make my way across the landing and into the bathroom. The bathroom at my parents' house isn't very big but behind the door there is another, smaller room that was often dark because of the floor to ceiling shelving and the boiler cupboard at the far end. My friends used to hate going to the bathroom and would swiftly move beyond that small room to escape the feeling of being watched. In my dream that night I stood in the main bathroom space and an old and grotesquely ugly lady emerged from that smaller room. She was short and covered in moles that framed a mouth full of dark and broken teeth. She was dressed like a goblin and looked essentially like a fairy-tale witch. I wasn't scared of her, but her message was very clear. She demanded that I write a poem in the next three days and the moment she had delivered her instruction, I woke. The next night I wrote that poem and it was called 'The Elephant Mother'. It was the first poem I had written that came right from the heart and I saved many copies of it along with a framed hard copy that was a gift from Sazzle one year. The copies have been lost over time and the framed copy that once stood proudly on a shelf in my office eventually found its way into a storage box and a resting place in the loft. I came across the box a few years back and the frame was empty. I have no idea how or why, but maybe the old lady has taken it for herself. Either way that dream was responsible for putting the first seed of poetry in my blood and once there, I couldn't ignore it.

Poetry was never easy and I had to be driven by something to do it. I found poetry more difficult than anything else I had tried. I wanted to dance and I wanted to sing and yet I always seemed to end up writing in some way, shape or form. It was always about words. I even had my own comic as a child. It was called *Thunderpuss*. It was meant to be a spinoff of *Thunder Cats*. With the benefit of hindsight, I can't see that it would ever have worked. *Thunderpuss*? Really, Christopher? What was I thinking? I made a comic about superhero cats sound more like a cheap porn film! I wrote diaries all the time, diaries that I still have and often dip read just to entertain myself with how dramatic I was back then. Really, I should have been an actor.

I loved the English language yet poetry was and still is a challenge. I would spend days and nights being drawn back by a half-written poem and would be unlikely to write any more than one or two in a whole year due to the sheer effort. I never did it to please anyone else or for praise, but they had to be perfect to me. I was so frustrated by my own creative indecision that my spark started to go out; maybe I wasn't creative after all.

When I was twenty-one I experienced my own revolution of reality. I wanted a proper job. I wanted to wear a power suit and work in a state-of-the-art office block in the city. I had started work a few years earlier in a local department store but the life of a bathroom installation complaints advisor was not for me. I remember one day spending so much time on tap faults that I answered the phone as a bath tap, 'Morning, bath tap, how can I help?' Unwilling to let that minor lapse in concentration go, my lovely friend Sazzle arranged for her mum to call the store and to ask to speak with the bath tap. Luckily I answered the phone fully alert and I replied, 'That's me, how can I help you madam?' I recall one complaint involving a toilet being fitted in a space that was too small for the lady of the house to sit down. Unfortunately, when we had sent the fitters around to measure the space, they measured the wall, floor and everything else you would expect, but had strangely enough not measured her ass, and her ass had then become my problem. I was not going to spend my working life talking about taps, toilets and oversized ass, so after that job and a short stay in the Royal Mint, I set my sights on the big city. No, not London, but Cardiff. A boy has to start somewhere, after all!

So be careful what you wish for, you might just get it. Before I reached twenty-two, I had made it as far as my office dreams were concerned. I was a medical insurance advisor in a small but very busy call centre. It was a new office block located directly opposite the city prison. Walking to work was always interesting thanks to the inmates and whatever abuse they wanted to shout from the cells that morning. 'Office boy wanker!' was my personal favourite, followed by 'Oi Oi Gay Boy'. In all honesty I was fairly impressed; I mean how did they know? I walk butch, look butch, talk butch… right? Maybe it was the man bag that did it. Damn you, Louis Vuitton! What was really funny is that once I got over the fact that it wasn't personal I almost looked forward to the attention. In fact, on days when I failed to get a single abusive comment I almost felt neglected. I would always wave and smile back and the dark grey walls, not with a sense of arrogance but with a genuine fondness for their creative efforts in the language department. One morning one inmate even used the word penis instead of dick, which I thought was a sophisticated evolution of our dialogue. After the first few years the abuse stopped. Someone who failed to appreciate it clearly complained and the good old days were over. After that, the only sound that left the prison was the odd wolf whistle. I assumed that was always for someone else, but hey, who knows? Maybe I had an admirer from behind the steel bars.

Inside the office I wore a Madonna-style headset on a daily basis. I may have been sat at a desk and not on the stage in Wembley but when nobody was looking I would daydream away and get transported to another world where I was belting my way through my opening number to a packed crowd. This was often rudely interrupted with a loud notification ping that told me a call was coming through, 'Good morning this is Christopher, how may I help you?' At least I was answering as myself and had ditched the bath tap alias.

The French Connection

So I was twenty-two, officially a very important and busy city worker, I encountered dangerous criminals every day and won and most importantly I had learned how to attend a serious morning meeting while being severely hung-over.

I had moved out from home and now lived in Cardiff with a group of friends. Our house was smarter than the average house share. We had a newly refurbished terraced house near Roath Park with a nice big garden that was perfect for impromptu parties. The house was made up of Tracey, Nicola, Sazzle, Rhoda and me. Tracy escaped the name-changing tradition but Nicola was also fondly known as Trott, which was in fact her surname. But not satisfied with the mere use of her surname, Nicola had to further re-brand. We lived very near to a part of the city known as Splott, which was by anyone's standards shady, and the fact that Splott rhymed with Trott was just too good an opportunity to miss! And so, one distinctive night, in between rounds of flaming sambuca, Nicola not at all surreptitiously announced with a shriek of pure self-congratulation, that from that day forward she would be known not as Trott from Splott but instead as the very regally promoted, Lady Tro from Splo! We laughed so hard that night, and despite marriage, parenthood and twenty-plus years of distance, Nicola will always fondly be Lady Tro from Splo to me.

We had such good times there, including the day we decided to play drinking games all afternoon before hitting town. In normal circumstances that would have been fine, but this was a Sunday! Nicola was our party girl and didn't really take no for an answer. Already worse for wear we taxied into town and rocked up at the first bar. Nicola being Nicola, she had recruited our first new friend by the time we had ordered the first drink. Anyone who looked remotely interesting or appeared to be on their own didn't stand a chance when Nicola was around and they were very swiftly welcomed into the brood for one night only. Some may have called it temporary adult-napping, but we all liked to think of it as community service. Anyway, this night Nicola had picked a good one. We had ambushed the lovely but slightly bemused hairdresser of Cherie Blair. There was a political party conference in Cardiff and Tony was in town with Mrs Blair. We showed him what a night out in Cardiff was all about after a series of interrogations relating to No. 10, bad hair and what it was like to work for the lovely Cherie. We ended that night in an Irish bar drinking Guinness by the pint. The next morning, each and every member of the house had to do the walk of shame down to the local telephone box to call in sick with a series of well thought out illnesses. For a number of reasons, we named that day Black Sunday. Knowing how we all felt that day, I dread to think of how poor Cherie's hair looked that morning. More first beast than first lady, I'm sure.

Another unforgettable night became known simply as The Party. We had selected a handful of people each to invite for a house-warming and so expected a fairly lively but pleasant affair. A few started to arrive, and then a few more, and then a few more. In less than two hours the house was full and looked more like a nightclub on a Saturday night. From front to back you could see a sea of heads, and only fifty per cent of those heads had any link to us. We started to panic as we made our way through the rooms, trying hopelessly to regain some control. There was sex in the bathroom and garden, drugs being shared in the toilet and vodka snorting over the kitchen sink. It was official – we were out of control and remained so until the police arrived. At the time we were mortified, but in retrospect the police arriving was the best thing that could have happened. We had been saved, even if it did result in an eviction warning.

It wasn't long after that time that Nicola introduced me to J. J was to be my first real adult, full on, not-pretend boyfriend. Despite being very unsure of J at the start, he made me laugh, and he was endearing and intelligent. I had spent so much time not interested in anyone and then in almost the blink of an eye, I fell in love. I had no reference point and no possible way of preparing for the mind space love can claim. I was snagged hook, line and sinker, and in that moment, those first few months and years, every other ambition, hope or desire just quietly disappeared.

I came out to my family and packed my creative ambitions away in a make-believe shoebox labelled 'Not now', but I was happy. Coming out to my folks was easier than I had expected. It was Christmas Eve and my mum was peeling the vegetables for Christmas dinner the next day. I was sat opposite my mum in the sitting room and I was reading the *Christmas Radio Times*. Christmas music was playing through the TV and the fire was on, sending waves of warmth over my feet as I floated them about playfully in front of me. There was meat cooking and the smell had already found its way out of the kitchen and into my nostrils. That and the smell of fresh paint was always a sign that it was Christmas in our house. My mam would issue paint orders to my dad every year in early autumn, and every year the paint jobs were done in the days leading up to Christmas Eve, so you see to me Christmas is as much gloss and emulsion as it is mince pies and turkey.

I could sense that there was something on my mother's mind. It was the same room where I had learned to first write my name all those years earlier, the same room where my cardboard washing machine had been brought to life, and where I have thrown myself on the floor in a net curtain pretending to be in the 'Like A Virgin' video. It was a little room full of happy memories and I guess it was time to make a new one. From the silence the words appeared, direct and to the point. 'So are you gay?' my mother asked. I was a little bit stunned, like a bird that had just been clipped by a car. Thankfully, I managed to stay upright in the chair and wasn't stiff on my back with my legs in the air. I started to lower the *Radio Times*, revealing my best steely and unbothered face, which would hopefully disguise the most awkward and totally bothered mind. I wasn't ready, and so I was considering an answer that wouldn't be a lie but was also not the exact truth, but before I could think my mother had spoken again to justify her question and it went something like this:

'It's just that I found your Christmas gift list and you have spent the same amount on all of your friends except the boy whose name I don't recognise. You have spent five times as much on him.'

With my game plan now dramatically weakened by two points to nil in my mother's favour, I surrendered.
'Well I never used to be,' I said.
'But you are now?' she replied.
'Yes, I am.'
'Well you had better tell your father.'
'Well I will.'
'Good.'
'Good.'

I put down the magazine neatly on the arm of the chair and stood to leave the room. I had made a couple of steps towards the hallway door and the escape was going well and I was still alive, hadn't been swallowed into the floor and my mother still hadn't passed out or become hysterical so all in all it was going well.

'Um, so who is he?' my mother said.

Oh no! I had almost made it to neutral ground. I had been on the home run to the safety of my bedroom where I could have paced for an hour, stuck my head in the pillow and pulled a few strange faces in the mirror which is something I seemed to do when I was nervous. But no, my mission was aborted and round three commenced.

Christmas Day came around and it felt like nothing had changed. We ate breakfast as a family, opened our gifts, collected my grandmother and settled down for the usual banquet followed by napping and the Queen's Speech. It must have been the word queen that had reminded my mother of my now twenty-four-hours-old revelation! Bloody Queen! I helped collect the teacups and followed my mam into the kitchen to help with the washing up:

'So have you told your Father?'
'Not yet,' I said. 'It's Christmas Day and I need to prepare for what I am going to say. I have given it a lot of thought and I am almost ready, maybe Boxing Day after lunch.'
'Well don't think too hard, I have already told him,' she said.
'What?'
'Don't look so worried. He was okay, he said it didn't change anything, you were still Christopher. He has a few other questions but nothing major.'
'What other questions?'
'Nothing really, he just asked if you liked cross dressing.'
'What? What has that got to do with me being gay?'
'Well you did used to like to wear a blanket as a dress.'
'Oh my lord, I used to like Sue from the *Sooty Show*, it doesn't mean I am a raving heterosexual puppet pervert! Anyway, it wasn't ever a dress, it was a cape, I was being Darth Vader!'
'Oh okay, right you are.'

The conversation didn't last that much longer and after my initial interview I entered into a period of bi-daily cross-examination. I expected it and actually, on a more serious note, I know that my parents deserved that time to get their heads around it. That Christmas was a little different, but not dramatically so, and life went on. Just for the record, at that point in my life I loved men's fashion and had no desire to express myself in any other way, not that I wouldn't have embraced it had I wanted to. I mean, yes, okay, there was some truth in the blanket story but I was six for God's sake. Surely, I wasn't the only impressionable young boy blown away by the grandeur and splendour of Charles and Diana's wedding.

The royal wedding. I was peeled to the screen, literally unable to miss a moment. I remember my school friend Brian knocking on the door halfway through the service! I opened the door and stared in amazement, what was he thinking? Did he even have a TV? I abruptly shared my shock that he would even think that I could go out to play at a time like this and closed the door, taking my little feet back across the hall and into the lounge so that order could resume. It was my first royal wedding, and it was like pure magic and truth be told, I did wrap myself up in a rather large quilt and descended our staircase in a bid to recreate the scene of Princess Diana leaving St Paul's Cathedral. A significantly large quilt had been on the edge of the bed, looking a little ruffled, and as I walked past it caught my attention and instantly I was transported back to that big blousy frock. Not having the means to ask Dave or Lizzy Emanuel for a copy I decided it would be fun and an all-round excellent idea to wrap myself in it and re-create the wedding finale! Unfortunately, the quilt was huge and I was not, and so after catching my feet for the third and final time I very ungracefully tumbled in a twisted heap down the last three steps, landing in the soft protection of my lovely wedding dress.

I was a lucky lad when I came out. Not only did my parents support me, but my brothers were also spectacularly good about it. It feels almost antique in its thinking now, but even back then in 1996, where I came from coming out wasn't easy. I was one of the lucky ones, but some people never came out. They chose to pretend, to do the 'right' thing, to not bring shame on their families and to not join the revolution of freedom. Some did none of that and decided that all options were too painful, and so instead of taking the road less travelled they decided to take their own lives. My parents' biggest worry for me initially was that I would get ill. They had been frightened just as much as I had by the AIDS outbreak and by the portrayal of it in the media. I've said it before and I will say it again, it wasn't self-inflicted ignorance but ignorance at the hands of monsters who knew better and who made a choice to use the AIDS epidemic to promote their own beliefs that gay people were diseased, condemned and destined for hell. If you are sitting comfortably in 2021 and reading this thinking: really? Well yes, really. The person who ran this country at that time in the early 80s was outspokenly and unashamedly homophobic, and some of her youngest disciples are still around in government today, but a little 'outwardly' warmer, shall we say, to the concepts of equality!

To my face, my parents were exactly what I needed: loving, supportive and the most important thing of all for any child coming out, is that they were normal. They made 'it' normal, and that in itself makes 'it' go away. It makes the bombshell, the freak factor become nothing, it robs the fear of its fuel, and that is where confidence starts. Behind closed doors and away from me, however, I know that they had to work through it. I know my mam cried and I know that she was scared. My brother had to get HIV leaflets and sit with her, and explain and give her helpline numbers so that she could get answers. I hate that the world did that to my parents, I hate that they had to think those awful things, but I love them so much for protecting me from it. For my dad, he just couldn't see a life without kids, and while we all know now that being gay doesn't take that opportunity away, back then it kind of did. It wasn't a judgement but a worry. He couldn't imagine life without his kids and for him that was what life was all about, its most rewarding gift.

Over the years that followed I worked my way up through the company. My partner and I bought a house, and then a bigger house, then an even bigger house and so on. We travelled the world and I became settled in my blue-tie ambitions. My partner and I had started to consider the potential of buying a tiny house in France where we spent time each summer with his parents. They lived in a beautiful barn conversion and we would normally take over the farmhouse and sometimes the gîte with a tribe of friends we would go with once or twice a year.

All three properties overlooked a large courtyard that led onto the pool and the gardens that looked over a vast and beautiful stretch of French countryside. France became a second home to me: an escape and a sanctuary. When the day-to-day stresses (or worse, the day-to-day monotony) crept in, a trip to France was never far away and I loved being there. It felt like home. I remember the hot sunny days and long bike rides around the sunflower fields. I remember trying to talk French at the market and stopping for a café au lait in the town square before rushing back for lunch al fresco and a lazy afternoon by the pool. My favourite days would either be kayaking with a picnic down the river or visiting the pretty local towns like 'St Émilion' and Aubaterre. We would wander aimlessly around the cobbled streets stopping only for a cool drink or for me to buy yet another baby grape vine, which I would eventually kill off back in the UK. At night, we would sit on the terrace and drink French beer and red wine under a sky that was exploding with stars. There were no lights for miles around and so from the terrace there was no competition for the stars and so they dazzled. Food was always incredibly good and like everyone else who visits France, I always ate far too much bread and cheese. We were always spoiled for great restaurants but my favourite was The Chateau. It wasn't just a Chateau by name but was in fact a restaurant within an impressive seventeenth-century castle that overlooked the town of Chalais from a vantage point high on the cliff top. To enter the restaurant you had to cross a creaky wooden drawbridge and walk through a vast and beautifully kept courtyard. The walls of the interior were bare grey stone that formed large domed rooms with small arched doorways that led into a small labyrinth of private dining areas. There were elegant stone fireplaces that towered above the tables and magnificent fresh flower displays in every room. The whole restaurant was lit by candlelight and the atmosphere was always sophisticated but warm and the service always exceptional. The proprietor was charming and eager to please and would often talk me through the menu, explaining some of the dishes that were only ever presented in French on the menu. I would make the odd faux pas and he would often just smile and correct me in the politest and most discreet way. It was a special place and they were beautiful times.

I was now in the second half of my twenties and there was so much to be happy about. I had great friends, work was rewarding, I was financially stable and my family were all well and close to hand. A few tiny cracks had started to appear in my relationship but at that point there was far too much good to give these small fractures much thought. In fact, they were dismissible on the grounds that the honeymoon period had probably just ended and we were reaching a different stage of our lives together. Work was going well and we had settled into a beautiful new house that overlooked the sea in the land of *Gavin and Stacey*. It was a semi-detached new build town house built on the grounds of a once-thriving Butlins campsite. Despite an aged and out-of-date negative perception, Barry Island was and could be a beautiful place with a special energy all of its own. This was before Nessa's time, and yet I will always be proud to say that I once lived in a place that is now a Welsh legend. It's true that if you looked for it, you could find the odd slot machine arcade and a dodgy pub, but it was only ever really busy on a hot, sunny day and if truth be told a hot, sunny day in Wales is a rare gift, so most of the time the island was peaceful and abandoned, to the benefit of its new residents. J and I were in that moment close to perfect, we literally had it all and I didn't just love him, I loved us, our family and our life. I wouldn't have swapped being me for anything else in the world.

Most of my friends at that time were somehow involved in aviation, either ground based or cabin crew. It felt like I spent a lot of my time listening to the life and times of the people who worked at Cardiff International Airport. Two of my neighbours, Craig and Martyn, became close friends, Craig was cabin crew and Martyn managed airport ground operations. Some, if not all, of the best memories of Barry were related to times spent with those two guys. Martyn was more sensible and practical and Craig was a louder, larger-than-life, flamboyant character who wore more make-up than a beauty counter consultant. It is fair to say that they made life interesting. In fact, I would go so far as to say that Craig and Martyn weren't just friends and neighbours, they were the local entertainment committee! But I loved them both.

Work was good, but I had itchy feet and fancied doing something completely different. With a bit of gentle persuasion, I applied for a role with BMI Baby. The airline was new and was famous for its bold red uniform, more specifically the Michelin jackets. I drove to the interview in London not having a clue what to expect, but what

I had not prepared myself for was an X-Factor style audition that would last eight hours. I joined a group of around fifty people and we were put through a series of challenges, one after another, and then at the end of each stage ordered to go into one of two rooms. One room would be full of those being sent home and the other full of those staying for the next challenge. It was funny at first, but as the day developed it began to get all a bit boring. Craig had said to me, just smile and you'll be fine, and so I did. I smiled all day. At times I had to go to the toilet just to not smile, and strangely enough they were the only moments that actually did make me want to smile. Smiling on request was never something I did, so on that day I am sure that I used up my whole annual smile allowance – I may have smiled so much that my ability to smile has never been quite the same since. Craig was right, though, of course. I smiled my way to the job offer.

Six weeks later, I packed up my headset and office desk and made my way to London to start my six-week training course to become a trolley dolly. I learned advanced first aid and became much better acquainted with Resus Annie than I wanted to. I despised messing about with that doll, and yet it went on forever, it seemed. We were practically in a relationship by the time training ended! I slid down aircraft slides, jumped in and out of rafts in Olympic-sized swimming pools, dragging fellow trainees around in life jackets, and all in all it was amazing fun. Then there was the job itself. I hated it. There's no other word for it. The hours were long, the routine was boring and once the performance of the safety demo was over it was always a big anticlimax. Crew get a hard time from passengers who often assume they are all a bit stupid, mere waiters in the air, but I have to say that some of the passengers I encountered were some of the stupidest people I have ever met. I remember one lady asking me during a busy flight if there was any fresh fish available, 'None of this pre-prepared rubbish if you can help it, dear.' In the absence of a fresh fish counter in the cockpit, maybe she thought I could go back to the galley to pull out my 35,000-foot fishing rod in the hope of passing over a handy salmon farm! I patiently explained that the chicken sandwich had been prepared that day and that was all I could offer at that exact moment. Her reply was profound. She said, 'Dear boy, chicken is not fish.' You learn something new every day.

I think my clearest memory was the day a rather large lady came pounding down the aisle the instant the seat belt signs had gone off and shot into the toilet, slamming the door behind her with such force it almost fell off its hinges. Twenty minutes went by without a sound, then twenty-five minutes, and I knew what was coming and so I was willing her to make an appearance. Half an hour later, I had the lovely job of asking through the door, 'Madam, are you okay?' Nothing!

'Madam, if you don't answer I will have to try to come in to ensure you are safe and well.'

There was a ruffle and huff and the door swung open. 'Excuse me, but I will come out when I am good and ready, unless you would like me to shit myself in the seat.' It wasn't said quietly, it was practically a public announcement. Within a second the door had shut again, and I smiled politely at the passengers, who were by this time staring at me, as if waiting for an official word on the situation. Forty-five more minutes passed and a number of 'Oh Gods' before the lady finally appeared again. She had gone in looking like a strong, robust and let's just say, ample woman, and came out looking like Gollum. She stumbled into the galley and said, 'I'm terribly sorry but I've had a bit of a blow-out.' A bit! From the other side of the wall it sounded like she was open cast mining. I thanked her for keeping me up to date on her progress and wished her a pleasant onward journey.

I persevered for a year, but on my anniversary, I hung up my gigantic red puffer jacket and vowed that only as a passenger would I ever fly again. That was a long time ago now, but still whenever I fly I can't help but assess the safety demonstration for pure presentation and performance value. I may have struggled with the whole smiling thing, but my safety demo was first class.

Despite my return to the city and my desk job we stayed on Barry Island for a few more years. I had started to run again and was running three/four times a week. I would do the coastal path. When you're running beside the sea with views like those sweeping around Jackson's Bay, suddenly exercise becomes an absolute pleasure. I would jump out of bed rain or shine and I would be out there in my running gear and my iPod and I loved it. I lost a lot of weight and started to feel really good. I had also discovered the Welsh wonder of Penderyn whisky at that point in my life and I recall only letting myself have one measure per weekend as a treat. It was also a way of warming up the blood in preparation for the next day's run. I read somewhere that single malt whisky had medicinal qualities, and who am I to argue with a doctor? If something tastes that good, can it really be that bad?

Liquid Gold

As bright as a star, as bold as brass
A glimmering statue demanding my stare
A notion to stand, to make the pass
Finding my feet I abandon the chair
Beneath the soft light, above the hard stone
So strong and demure, inviting me home

The liquid sparkles in its dazzling state
Pulling me closer to sample the pleasure
Taking my hand, claiming my fate
In a shimmering moment I discover the treasure
Strength finds the glass, a warrior in flight
From shadows it flows designing the light

A seduction of scent, so gentle, so sweet
A surrender of notion, a bringing to life
My lips let the kiss take in the heat
A passionate fire, a charm oh so rife
A velvet encounter, a beautiful start
A dragon now breathing gold into my heart

Now God

I am not sure if it was the sea air or the fact that I had started to feel good about myself for the first time in a long time, but I decided it was time to invest in something spiritual to round off what had become the holistic renovation of me.

I had always believed in God, and always felt the presence of something much greater from as far back as I can remember. I prayed in the conventional, predictable sense at very high and low points in my life, but I had never actually been religious. I had been to Sunday school and church services, but the truth was that for everything I agreed with there were always far too many rules or opinions that I couldn't accept, and so I could never really attach myself to any one belief system. Out of pure curiosity I tried to read the Bible as a young boy, but that never worked. It sounds dramatic now, but it didn't feel like it was meant for me, somehow, that I shouldn't even have been holding it in my hand, and so I always ended up putting it away. I think even at a young age I instinctively knew the Bible was a flawed translation that could generate darkness as well as light. I didn't just disagree with what I understood from its pages, I had a visceral sense that I shouldn't be reading it. One specific day I experienced something, almost like a sign. I'm fairly certain that it would have freaked most people out so I said nothing to anybody at that time and have only ever since told one person about it, but the incident was profound for me and after it happened I knew I had a different path to take. What I experienced was nothing dramatic in the physical sense, but it did happen, although I will never know if it was something I did to myself in my sleep or something more incomprehensible. It may not even feel dramatic to me now but it would be one of those things that very few people would ever believe, and so to preserve my own integrity and to not be that person that everyone looks at in silence while screaming bullshit with their eyes, I decided to simply always keep it to myself. No, I didn't see God in the clouds or Jesus at the foot of my bed! My brother once saw a ghost at the foot of my bed, but that's another story!

I am sure that we have all experienced some level of psychic activity at some point in our lives. We may acknowledge it or dismiss it as coincidence or simply a moment of silliness, but we have probably all had those moments in some form or other. I have had more than a few, some more real than others, and I no longer need to be convinced of the link that exists between the physical world and the spirit world. I have felt it, seen it and respect it. One of the milder experiences I had was with a white feather. I was painting a wall in my bedroom on the second floor of the house, and so there was an empty floor between me and J, who was sitting in the lounge with the fur children, watching TV. It was about 10 p.m. and I had been painting for only a short time. I remember starting to feel fidgety and I found myself stopping and looking around at the empty room every few minutes. I turned the radio off because I can't listen to anything if I am agitated. I carried on painting but started to feel uncomfortable because of a nagging feeling that I wasn't on my own. The room was built into the attic space of the property to create a three-level town house, and the staircase circled from the first floor beyond a private door right into the middle of the bedroom floor. The staircase wall was fairly long but there was a window alongside it that let in a lot of light during the day. I don't know why, but I felt the need to walk the lamp to the top of the stairs and to shine it into the corner where the staircase met the bedroom floor. As I turned to go back to the paint, which was on the opposite wall, I saw a large white feather resting in the middle of the carpet. I had no reason to suspect a thing. I mean, so what? A white feather. But then I picked it up and instantly I knew it meant something, and I was also fairly certain it wasn't there when I walked away from the wall five seconds earlier. I was chilled, the hairs stood on end all over my body. That sensation has almost become a truth detector to me over the years. If my body gives me no sign, then whatever I am experiencing is probably not true, but if it's real I get a feeling of cold energy raising up through my legs, and the energy moves up through my body until every hair feels like it is standing on end. That is what happened in that moment, holding the feather. I left everything as it was and made my way downstairs and out of the room as swiftly as my feet could carry me.

The next day we drove to Swansea to collect three paintings that I had commissioned to match the new bedroom colour scheme. Being so close to J's grandmother's house we had decided to call in for tea with Beryl. We had only just sat down with a cup of tea and the usual mountain of cakes and biscuits when Beryl said to me, 'Have

I ever told you about the white feathers?' My heart almost stopped, and then started beating faster than it should. I couldn't believe what I was hearing. Beryl went on to tell me that a white feather is a sign that your spirit guide or guardian angel is close by, either to simply be close to you or to protect you. Beryl went on to say that you might see a feather blowing about on the street that doesn't necessarily mean anything, but if you find a feather that is meant for you then you will instinctively know it. She said no matter where it appears your gut will always tell you if it means something. I couldn't resist and expecting her to be amazed I told her about the night before. She wasn't amazed. In fact, Beryl was very calm and said, 'Christopher, the feeling of not being alone last night was either due to the fact that you could sense that your guardian angel was there with you or there was something else in that room with you and the feather was there to indicate that your guardian angel was there to protect you from whatever it was. Either way, you shouldn't let that frighten you.' I left stunned. Surely that could not have been a coincidence. I still have that feather, but hopefully not the visitor that initiated its appearance that night, if that is what it was.

When I was a teenager people had stopped talking about religion but hadn't really started talking about other forms of spirituality. In the late 80s it almost felt like there was a void. God and religion had almost become taboo in young social circles; it just wasn't relevant or cool. I never really brought it up with anyone, not because I was bothered about it not being relevant or cool, but because it was a personal subject and something that I felt protective of. If I thought the people around me would just think it was all a pile of crap, then I wouldn't extend the invitation for them to say so. If I was ever prompted to share my views, however, then I would without hesitation and always have.

I had started to study Kabbalah. I had read *The Way* by Rav Berg and I liked what I read, and so I bought another book. One thing led to another and soon I had a London-based tutor and was spending about ten hours a week on my study and meditation. I started to feel my mind expand to take in new ways of looking at the world and new ways of looking at my own behaviour and the behaviour of those around me. I was convinced that I had at last found something that I belonged to, and at a time when this sense of belonging was still somehow important to me. Until that point prayer had always been to ask for safety or health for my family or to say a swift thank you for something that had worked out, but my whole perception of a relationship with a greater power of love now started to change. Prayer or meditation became about spending time in the stillness with whatever love energy was out there, the energy that I had felt and acknowledged throughout my life. Meditation was experiencing stillness in between the chaos of life and in that stillness I started to feel connected to that greater energy, something more powerful than I had ever experienced before. At times the meditation was so powerful I would have answers to questions that I knew to be true and I would start to pick up on energy in the house, especially in the room where I would spend time meditating in. It would occasionally unnerve me. As a teenager I was always aware that I needed to be careful with spirituality, to not go too far. I didn't know what that meant, really, but it was a pre-programmed warning that existed in my thoughts. I knew I could see and feel things that were not always easy to explain and sometimes you have to know when to stop, and also know when sharing what you feel or see isn't the best idea, unless you want to turn yourself into the local crazy man. My quest was to find something that made sense to me, but I never had any desire to delve further than I should, not back then anyway.

When I started to have a greater command of the belief system my tutor began to ask me about surrendering a percentage of my salary. I was already supporting aid work in Uganda with sponsorship of two children, so I suggested that my investment in that charity was achieving the same goal as any potential investment in the Kabbalah fund. We disagreed and I refused to be told how I should invest in charity and so the tutoring came to an end. Soon after my study reduced and only the meditation continued. A lot of what I still believe in is grounded in the Kabbalah principles but my relationship with the Kabbalah movement has for now ceased to exist. For many reasons I thought that was for the best. Kabbalah is said to be something that should only be studied by the most mature minds that can accept the truth, and because of that many men and women only ever scratch the surface by studying so late in life. That now makes a lot of sense to me, but even if I only scratched that surface I started to understand its power.

Over the years I have also encountered powerful personal and geographical spiritualism, spiritualism that has come from the energy of the people I have surrounded myself with at the time, 'birds of a feather', so they say. The years I spent in Swansea were by far the most spiritual; almost everyone I knew or met was in some way feeding my appetite for theology. J's sister was one of only two doctors in the whole world to hold a doctorate in NDE (Near Death Experiences) and from her time as an intensive care nurse, she established a passionate interest in death and the spiritual journey from life to the other side. Listening to the many stories and accounts that had been collected through the years of her study was fascinating, like picking up a great book that you couldn't put down. Through J's sister I was introduced to other people that I became greatly influenced by. One specific lady was the founder of a spiritual tolerance charity that pushed the message of love and tolerance amongst the world's religions so that children developed open, respectful minds and not hate for religious differences. The charity had done such amazing work to drive change through youth programmes and I started to help out in any small way that I could. I edited a video montage, I assisted with set-up planning for their youth awards and attended the odd meeting with local council directors to obtain support. It was at the youth awards that I met one of their patrons, Bonnie Tyler. She was still looking good as she rocked up in her sports car and I remember that she smelt really good, not that I was sniffing her of course, but we hugged for a photograph and the waft of scent that came my way was gorgeous. It wasn't only the great work being done that inspired me, it was also that the founder's conviction in making a difference was staggering. That in itself was such motivation to want to be part of it. I have always been drawn to strong, authoritarian women that have a fiery focus and a desire to pursue their goals, and that was this lady. There was another attribute I fondly identified with, and that was a sense of urgency, a sense of getting things done in the face of every obstacle. People don't always like that in a character and they mistake single-minded focus for being a diva, too demanding or simply being a bit of an overpowering bitch. You can call it what you like, but as Madonna once said, 'Sometimes you have to be a bitch to get things done.'

During my support of the charity I was introduced to a gentleman who shared an interest in starting a spiritual book club. We met for coffee one day to chat through our ideas and to establish if we were interested in the same type of thing. Now, I am an open-minded guy and it takes a lot to make me feel uneasy, but wow that meeting was uncomfortable. The guy started telling me how he had studied the life of the 'real' Jesus. Not the man presented in the tales from the Bible, but the real human being behind those stories. That sounded interesting, but my uneasiness came when he started to explain that he could see into his previous lives and how he and I must have been connected before. He was telling me about my aura and that we could never get along because I had no concept of who I really was and who I had once been, as if he knew. I finished my coffee and made my excuses. The strangest thing was that I had seen a green glow around his hands as he was speaking to me, like a mist. I knew that auras had colour, and as an active GP (Google Practitioner), I set about finding out about it on my mobile as I sat in the car outside the coffee shop. According to the Internet's leading authorities, this green aura could mean that he was a love-centred person or that he was jealous and full of resentment, almost a victim, depending (apparently) on the shade of green. As I couldn't remember the exact shade I erred on the side of positivity and awarded him the description of 'Love-Centred'. I was certain of one thing, however, and that was that in this life at least I wouldn't meet him again. That afternoon he left me pondering my views on reincarnation and what the hell I may have once been, but I soon shook that off under the realisation that sometimes just being me right now was enough of a challenge. I can't always remember what I had for breakfast in the morning, so my chances of identifying my past self was a tall order of Jack and The Bean Stalk size proportions. Also, I might not have liked what I found. It's my view that you have to be careful what you dig up when you reach for a spade, you might not find a diamond in the dramatic rough of time, instead you might stumble across a piece of coal in the shit, and on that lovely thought I surrendered all appetite.

My time in Swansea also saw my introduction to Adrian, who was also a friend of J's sister, and who I now realise, as I am writing this, was my spiritual pimp. Adrian was a Buddhist with flawless beliefs; he had the kind of passion that was so deeply rooted that you couldn't fail to be lifted by his spirit. Adrian was no Buddhist salesman, he was just a man that had found his path, and was proud to share it so that others could also experience the peace he had come to know. It was Adrian who explained the world of Nichiren Buddhism to me with great passion. I did read about it, attend meetings and I even hosted a chanting session at my house, but ultimately it didn't touch me or bring me any peace in the way it had for Adrian, and so I was left with no connection to the practice, but with a newfound respect. In fact, many years on I still find myself chanting, 'Nam – myoho – renge – kyo' at the oddest moments, and when I catch myself doing it, it makes me smile.

My favourite Swansea moment came in the form of my first 'journeying' experience. Journeying is a hypnotic journey that you take under the direction of (in my case) a white witch. I was attending a psychic day and in the final segment we had started a group journey that would see us all experience very different outcomes. I recall being led by the witch's voice along a corridor and through a door; it was all very *Alice in Wonderland*. When I twisted the knob and opened the door I detached from the voice and found myself in an open space with broad fields and mountains that were framed by tall grasses blowing in a gentle wind. In the distance there was a small clearing with an old bench and I found myself making my way there. When I arrived, I sat down and closed my eyes and started to breathe in the fresh country air. Within a moment I felt the sensation of being cradled around my back and looked up to see the most beautiful elephant towering above me. A feeling engulfed me, a very peaceful feeling of protection and sanctuary. The strong muscles of the trunk gripped against me, giving me the firmest reassurance that I was safe. It was such a real and special bonding moment. I sat for a while and stroked the beautiful creature in return for the affection she had shown me. I recall that after a short while I started to feel the need to return to the door. The elephant knew this and gently unwrapped me and as I stood to walk away I gave one last stroke to the elephant's trunk and started to make my way back through the brightest green grass. Just before I arrived back at the door I looked back and she was still there. I knew it was a 'she' and 'she' was still watching me. I opened the door and the voice in my head started to get louder until there was the audible instruction to open my eyes. I sat for a moment watching the other delegates and soon we had started to chat. The witch, whose name I no longer recall, called for order and sat down at the head of our now neatly formed circle before starting to speak. 'So, who brought the elephant back, because it's standing right here and it is quite a distraction, as you can imagine.' I was thinking, 'What, really?' The sceptic in me had woken up even though I had to admit it had been a very beautiful experience. As it turns out, as we worked our way around the room, I was the only person who had met an elephant. The name Suma was in my head and so while telling my little story I attached the name to her, being honest about the fact that it had just come into my mind. The elephant hadn't told me its name, obviously, because that would be silly and quite impossible right?

When I arrived home that night, I had an email waiting for me from a charity I had worked with in China. They were writing to confirm that they had commenced a new mission in Sumatra, taking care of orphan elephants. Suma, Sumatra! What are the chances? What I later learned is that if you ever have a chance to meet your spirit animal then you should, or if you have a hunch of what it might be then you should look up the nature of that animal because you may learn something about yourself. It's called your totem animal and mine was a lovely great big elephant called Suma.

A few years on from my time in Swansea, out of pure curiosity I attended a Quaker meeting in Brighton. It was the strangest concept to me: no speaker, no higher level of authority and no discussion. It was simply a meeting of silent spirits. I walked into the chamber, which was housed in a beautiful old property near the Brighton Lanes. The room was tall and clad with different shades of wood that surrounded freestanding chairs arranged in a number of large circles. I sat in a chair much like a school chair at the back of the room and watched people of all ages enter and select one of the simple seats without making a sound. When the time arrived the doors were closed and what commenced was an hour of silent prayer. I closed my eyes and then opened them, and then closed them and then opened them. I secretly watched people who were becoming more peaceful in their posture and more relaxed in their soft facial expressions. I started to experience a deep feeling of peace and respect for my fellow participants in what for me was an experiment. I, too, started to feel relaxed and peaceful as my mind drifted gently between thoughts of what I can only describe as light. It was almost as if there was an electric circuit running through the room and I was part of it and it was flooding me with peace. I was worried at first that the hour would drag, but it was over in a flash and suddenly people started to stretch and stand. I sat for a while, taking in how something so simple could be so powerful. I decided not to stay for the tea and coffee session that I was told follows each of these meetings but instead I walked slowly across the beachfront and back to my apartment. It was an amazing experience and one that I will one day return to. At last there was nothing I didn't like. No pressure, no noise, just peace to find light, amongst the energy of other human beings.

I had exhausted my curiosity in finding a path to God. I had chanted, read, prayed and meditated but it's funny how things turn out. In my quest to find a spiritual system that I could belong to, I found that for me there was no such thing but instead a very personal and independent relationship with God that no religion, system or belief could ever fully define. A relationship that had always been there, unwavering. I have felt that energy with me since my first thoughts, I was blessed from the beginning with what most human beings really crave most of all, and that is an absolute knowledge from inside out that through love we are not alone and that we are somehow vessels for letting light and love into this world. I also learned that the answer to most questions in life could be found in another question, a question we would all benefit from by asking ourselves more often, and that is, 'What would love do?' It sounds simple, but if you sit and challenge yourself in a moment of true reflection, you will find that the answer to that question is usually never easy, and the adoption of the advice you hear in your heart usually means tough decisions that challenge the ways we have been taught to think. So next time you are stuck, or you have a choice to make that will affect your world or those you love and respect, ask yourself truly and deeply, what would love do, and if you're brave enough you will hear the answer. Sometimes you have to be even braver to turn the answer into action. So I am not a nutcase, or a preacher, in fact I would encourage everyone to simply do what feels right for them, but I have felt God, I have seen God in the world around us and I have been confronted with that spectacular, indescribable energy of love and for me once it has been known, it can never be unknown.

Now God

Dismissing gravity I climb closer to the light
In its glory I withstand the sun and my spirit illuminates under its rays
I move yet higher through the clouds and they conspire to follow me

I am the never ending beginning and the forever
I am the wind changer, the ocean driver, the earth mover
I am the master shape shifter defying perfection, depriving definition

The greatest most dazzling crescendo has began
The one and only light that breathes life into the deepest, darkest heart now transcends beauty and space

The applauding energy is raging defining the everything from within the reductive nothing
The spectacular moment of now has arrived

I feel you now God

Bette & The Man Knickers

At some point just before my Kabbalah study started, I met Bette. Bette was to be my new partner in crime, my fun revival, the bad example that I was desperate to find, my drinking partner and an amazing friend. We had the best nights out and partied hard into the early hours, talking for hours and dancing until we couldn't speak from exhaustion and beer. We were Welsh and proud and both loved rugby (and the men that played it!) One Six Nations game we celebrated to the point that we could no longer communicate effectively. After many hours of celebratory pub-crawling, we entered a taxi; instead of going home we ordered it to the nearest gay nightclub for some early hours dancing. We never knew when to give up! On arrival at Exit, which was a cellar club in Cardiff that happened to be opposite another cellar club called Club X, we paid the taxi driver and climbed out, Bette to the left, me to the right. It was twenty minutes later that we realised that we had left the car via different doors and headed into two different clubs, both alone and both convinced that the other was following behind. We found each other in the end and agreed that maybe on that occasion dancing could wait for another Welsh win and in fact it was time for a Burger King and a stroll home to bed.

Bette was prone to the travel bug and we often joked and fantasised about heading off somewhere far away to do something a little crazy. The joke became a regular discussion and eventually it became a concrete plan. In August 2005 we left Cardiff International Airport to teach English in Xian, China.

To this day, that trip was probably the best experience that I have ever had and what made it more special was that I shared that time in China with Bette. When we first arrived, it was cold and misty and I was desperate to use the loo. Bette promised to wait outside the door for me and I hurried inside the gents. In seconds I had run back out, convinced that someone had stolen the toilets. In my ignorance I had no idea that the public toilets in Xian were in fact holes in the ground. I don't mean small holes, I mean huge holes, holes you wouldn't want to balance or hover over after a couple of drinks. We had spent weeks learning to speak Mandarin, with limited success, but had spent less time looking up public facilities!

Why would you think to? It wasn't the most promising start, but I lifted my jumper over my face to form a protective veil from the waft of stink and balanced beautifully. It was that or wet myself so I chose the dirty hole in the ground and relief. I remember vividly the look on Bette's face as I re-appeared, disgruntled and fuming after my ordeal. Bette's look was one of 'What have I done, I have come to a deprived part of China, on the other side of the world and my travel companion is Dame Shirley Anstee!'

Xian was a large, smoggy and sweaty city with an ever-present haze that never seemed to lift. The hot, sticky atmosphere would often give me a claustrophobic feeling, but it wasn't all bad. In fact, Xian had deep historic roots and was full of ancient architecture including its most famous residents, the Terracotta Warriors. The Warriors are located outside of the city but the city itself has beautiful pagodas like the Big Goose, an ancient forty-foot city wall that stretches eight and a half miles around the old city and a bustling Muslim Quarter. One afternoon off from school Bette and I cycled around the top of the cobbled wall. Looking up to the top from the safety of the ground, the cycle adventure didn't feel like such a great idea, but the forty-six-foot width of the wall gave us a sense of safety. On reaching the top we were less worried about hitting a cobble and tumbling over the edge, but it was more of a bone shaker than a pleasure for sure. That said, it was a pretty special thing to do and a pretty great afternoon.

The Muslim Quarter was equal in terms of its experience value. This is where we ventured for tourist-style retail therapy. Being someone who is always drawn to tacky tourist trinkets, the Muslim Quarter was at times a feast for the eyes, however, also being someone with a low tolerance of bad smells and ugly sights, I made sure our trips to the market were always fast paced. The streets were dirty and dark and there would be meat rotting in glass containers under the thick heat with no refrigeration, chickens and ducks kept in disgustingly small cages barely able to move and every now and then you would hear the screams of some domestic storm going on behind the closed doors of the fragile looking market houses. I can't say that any of my favourite memories of that trip were of the Muslim Quarter.

The weeks passed quickly, and after a few days my initial feelings of homesickness fell away and I was loving it. At first, I refused to share a dorm with two young American lads and demanded I stay with Bette, but lost that battle. The lads were from upstate New York with summer homes in the quintessential buzzy beach location of the Hamptons. Their next-door neighbour was Glenn Close and they socialised with her children at her house. However, claim to fame stories and wealth aside, my instincts to not want to share with them, turned out to be well founded! I learned that in week two the lads had stolen underwear from my bag and had carried out a lesson for the under fifteens on what the difference was between American and British man pants. Yes, my pants were hung up all over the top of the chalkboard for everyone to see, which they thought was hysterical. If it wasn't actually funny, I would have stayed pissed with them for longer than five minutes. They were fascinated by my underwear. They wore boxers with more material that a six-man tent per leg and I wore normal briefs – normal in my eyes, at least. They called them man knickers. It wasn't unusual for them to put a pair on and shimmy around pretending to be British with the most awful attempts at an accent. I didn't help that as their mentor, being from the Welsh Valleys the result was an accent that sounded like a mash up between Tom Jones and Dawn French's impersonation of Catherine Zeta-Jones. What a legacy to send back to the Hamptons. I wonder if my pants were ever discussed with Glenn Close over a Cabo on her front porch? In the end I grew fond of them both and I got used to my nickname (Chris Dog), and my pants being robbed and the underwear fashion shows at 2 a.m.. They weren't calling me an actual dog it appears; it was an actual term of American teenage endearment born from the Snoop Doggy Dog era and it is only awarded to someone 'cool' enough to be deserving of the title. So it was time to move over Rover, Chris Doggy Dawg was in the Haus! Well, the bottom left bunk at least!

My second diva demand came from the horrific shock of my first ever cold shower. I stormed out of the bathroom, shivering. I call it a bathroom; it was a room with no tiles and a broken floor, it had a bulb hanging from the ceiling that could barely light a trinket box, and a dirty curtain was all that separated the toilet space from the shower space. Apparently, it was designed so that different people could use the facilities at the same time. How very lovely. I stormed down to the house manager and demanded that they fix the shower, only to be told that it was not broken it was just a lower temperature than I was used to. He was of course correct in his choice of words

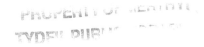

– it was colder than I was used to. I was used to heat and this was Jack Frost freezing… Battle two lost. Humph!

It was at that point Bette told me to buck up and stop being 'such a diva'. Bette had an open ticket to speak to me in any way she wanted without getting my back up. Bette was one of the few people in my life who could successfully put me in my place. I can't explain why that is, but Bette talks and I listen. Well, most of the time. But on this occasion, once again Bette was exactly right and so with my tail between my legs, I went into my tiny dorm room and threw some pants around, well the few that hadn't been stolen for educational purposes!

I wasn't in the greatest of moods and so I scowled at the boys for not hiding their vodka bottle very well and for making a general disaster zone of dirty clothes and towels. With a grumpy old face I lay on my bunk and realised that if I was being honest with myself then I was being a bit of a dick really and I needed to snap out of it. I was just getting into some seriously deep soul searching when a pair of boxer shorts hit me in the face, followed by the howls of laughter that you would expect from two nineteen-year-olds that had just successfully landed a pair of boxer shorts onto the face of the grumpy British guy they had to share their room with. My anger lasted as long as it had taken to pull them off my face. Instead of deep contemplation I had entered yet another three-way debate on crazy British fashion that left my sides aching from listening to their theories on how underwear could change your life. In that moment that one pair of boxers had at least changed my mood.

After my laughter therapy and having remembered that 'We weren't in Kansas anymore, Toto' I did human up and got on with it. As the days passed I learned so much about not just myself but the spoiled western society I was part of. I was generalising, but it was true. Excessive, grand luxury to some was everyday essentials to others. It is amazing how swiftly I adjusted and how very soon I forgot how pathetic I was being. I started to fall in love with the experience, every last bit of it, and I learned that as (clichéd as it is) the very best things in life really are free.

One of my fondest memories was English Corner. Chinese students used a square in the centre of the city to meet and chat with

American and British volunteers on a Thursday night to improve their English. The students would approach you and start discussions about anything and everything and they were not just grateful for your time, they were interested in everything you had to say and would respond with broad smiles and such enthusiasm. It started slowly, with one or two small groups walking curiously around the large marble square looking a little afraid and unconfident, but in no time at all there was a mass of students all fighting to be the next one to speak with you. Though overwhelming in moments, it was such a buzz. Soon I had forgotten that I was there to help them because the conversations developed into two-way interchanges about life and culture. I learned so much from them and they probably learned nothing new from me. I could have stayed there forever, but I had a class of five-year-olds the next day, so as the numbers started to slowly dwindle, I set off to bed.

My five-year-olds were the funniest little human beings I have ever met. They were like all five-year-olds in terms of energy levels but far too excitable to take a proper interest in my carefully prepared English lesson and therefore I decided to resort to teaching by song. By the end of the second week my class could belt out 'Twinkle Twinkle Little Star' better than a male voice choir from the Valleys. If you ever hear a full rendition of 'Twinkle Twinkle Little Star' while visiting Xian, then that was my doing, and you are welcome. It was impossible to not become attached to their little faces, so incredibly eager to see you every morning. From time to time I wonder what they are all doing now and pray that they made it out of poverty and succeeded in becoming strong, educated grown-ups with a future ahead of them. I just hope that those grateful little faces that used to welcome us with cheers every morning and send us off in our minibus with relentless hand waving every night are safe. Above all other things, I hope they are happy. They touched my spirit and I will never forget them.

Leaving Xian was hard. It had been so character building and such a gift, and I met some amazing people and experienced enough to write a short book just about that trip. The blow of having to leave was softened by flying to Beijing for a few days so that we could adjust before heading back to the UK. We had taken off from a dark, grimy city and landed in the city of the future. In the taxi my eyes were peeled to the sights of futuristic skyscrapers and the beautiful

Olympic stadium, which did in fact look like a giant bird's nest. As the taxi ploughed at speed through the city David Bowie's 'Changes' came on the radio and I can't to this day tell you why but I was overwhelmed with the whole experience, I looked over at Bette at my side, who was also looking out of her window and I thought of home, the kids we left behind in Xian and from behind my sunglasses I remember tears losing their place and running down my face. It was a moment I now relive every time I hear that song, a song that has definitely found its way onto the soundtrack of my life. In Xian, Bette and I had stepped into another world, and we had helped, but I felt almost like a fraud for leaving everyone we had met there behind and heading back to all of our luxury and privilege. I felt pulled away, bereft, tired and a bit lost, but that's exactly what this stopover in Beijing was meant to address and so I surrendered to bed at the hotel and cried a bit more until I woke the next morning. The next day felt different. My mood was not bright, but it was brighter, and we owed it to each other to get out there and see China and so we did.

In two short days we visited the Great Wall, the Winter Gardens and Tiananmen Square where we were stopped and asked to pose for photographs with eager Chinese teenagers. It was all very strange but very sweet. It wasn't because they thought we were famous, it was just something the local kids did when they saw people from the West, especially younger people. The whole trip was full of sweet moments like this; it was more than sweet; it was a special time. People tend to miss places and people, but I often miss that whole experience. Even though we see each other when we can, I will always miss Bette and that solid period of time we spent together in China.

Nothing felt the same after China for me. Not for a long time, at least. After the initial novelty of seeing J and my friends and family who welcomed us home with a house party, I fell into a sleepy few months of adjustment and reflection.

Daisies & Monsters

A few months after I returned home it was my thirtieth birthday. My closest mates and I rented a farmhouse near the famous market town of Hay on Wye. We picked it for its position in the beautiful mid-Wales countryside, miles away from civilisation. At first the novelty of having cows and sheep milling around the garden and the feeling of being away from the world was great, but we also discovered that it had its drawbacks.

On the first night we drank wine, sang songs, listened to music and munched our way through copious amounts of buffet food. We all went to bed feeling less than stable and more than full, but it did mean that we were all out for the count and all had a solid night's sleep. The next day we strolled through the small, charming market town of Hay, which is world famous for its book festival. We drank tea and ate scones with fresh cream and locally produced strawberry jam. We made our way back to the house early enough to prepare a hearty evening meal and all got stuck into the social pleasures of group cooking, drinking and ghost story telling. Maybe it was the ghost stories that tipped the somewhat vulnerable balance but let's just say the second night was a lot less peaceful than the first. At around 1 a.m. I started to hear noises in the wall, like the sound of small creatures hurtling through the cavity. I put up with it for a while but it appeared to be getting closer and closer (and when I say I put up with it for a while, it was probably less than ten seconds). Then I heard it right behind my head. I shot up in the bed and grabbed around for the pull cord of the light above my head. Eventually the light was on and I was sitting up inspecting the room. I looked in every corner but found nothing and so settled back into bed and I lay there with one eye still open and on high alert. A few moments passed and then, scratch, scratch, scratch, it was back, only this time the noise was coming from the ceiling as well as from the wall behind the bed. Oh Christ, there were two! I jumped up and flew across the landing to the girls, leaving J behind, who at this moment was both unsympathetic and useless, and fast asleep. I'm not sure my feet touched the carpet. I had thought the girls would be much braver and more likely to have some success in any battle against the beasts, but as it turned out we were all equally terrified and after a few failed attempts to appoint a brave human being to face the monsters, it was agreed that group force was the only reasonable answer. We decided to do the next best noble thing to hunting down the attackers, which was to hide. What that entailed in practical terms was that we all dragged our bedclothes into the girls' room and tried to sleep on the floor, filling up every space. At last, safety! It was now 3 a.m. and there were twelve eyes wide open and peeping over drawn up bedcovers. Every moment it became peaceful someone would shout out, 'Oh no there it is again,' usually followed by a scream or six. Had we not convinced ourselves that we were going to be set upon by the unknown beasts if we opened the bedroom door, we would have packed up and driven home there and then, but we decided to sit it out.

The sun came up and as fear turned to laughter, we all fell asleep for what must have been forty-five minutes. It's funny how pathetic the darkness of night makes you and how dismissive and brave the light of day. In the early hours the creatures could have been small wolves but over breakfast they had been demoted to mice. Whatever they were, I loved the fact that as the sun had come up they had settled down for a lovely long rest. Bless them. Little Fxxxxxs!

Things got back to normal and a few more years passed. In 2010 I lost one of my favourite people in the whole world, my grandmother. The only positive I could take from that loss was the time I spent with my aunty Susan, who I loved so much as a child but hardly ever saw due to the fact that my aunt, uncle and my cousins all lived in Worcester. People had always said that I looked like my aunty as a child and I remember her always having such a warm and pretty face, so although as a small boy I didn't really want to look like a girl I was happy to accept this as a compliment. On the days leading up to her death we spent a lot of time together and talked more than we had for years. In fact when my aunty eventfully left for home after the funeral, I was almost a bit bereft for her company as well as for my grandmother's passing.

My grandmother's death had a major impact on me. It was gut-wrenching. I had a call from my mum late in the evening and had rushed to the hospital, I wasn't sure what I was wearing when I got there and I had no memory of the journey but she was still alive, thank God. I sat there with my mum, my aunt and my brother and we stayed there all night. She woke briefly and my brother and I lifted her gently because she was reaching out to us. It was natural impulse to help her, to lift her, but as swiftly as she opened her eyes, her eyes closed again and so we laid her back on the mountain of pillows that were keeping her comfortable. Night turned to dawn and the morning to afternoon. I was thirsty and my aunt and I agreed to take a walk for coffee. We sat in the hospital canteen and I said, 'I don't feel like I need to be here anymore.' I thought no more of it and intended to walk back to her private room to kiss her goodbye. As we walked the corridor I saw my mother and brother outside the room and there were tears falling down my mum's face. She had gone; in that moment we had left she had slipped away almost like she had heard me in the coffee room.

On the day of the funeral I couldn't really get my head around what it would be like not having her in mind and body in this world. I felt like one of the anchors that had secured me to this earth had been cut and I had lost a little bit of my own identity. That may sound overly dramatic, but she had a big influence on my life, she was part of what made my life safe, part of my foundations. I sat in the front of the mourner's car on my own, I couldn't be comforted and nor did I want to be. I shed no tears and I rarely spoke. I arranged for J to travel in a different car and I fell into a world and a space all of my own for the whole of the service and for most of that day.

I have often asked my grandmother what I should do in moments of my life that have been difficult for whatever reason, and in one way or another I always get the answer, even now. I know one thing for sure and that is that she is still with me. I don't just think it, I absolutely know it.

Sweet Daisy May

If a beautiful daisy was simply a lady
That sparkled and bloomed with delight
Then that daisy may show me a secret, bestow me
With love like a sparkling light

Wise strength but so dainty my sweet pretty daisy
Petals that cwtch to her heart
A smile full of sunshine so full from a lifetime
A kindness that set her apart

My sweet daisy did flutter as the winds danced around her
But she always stood tall in her place
Always there to be found, always beaming so proud
Of the daisies that grew by her grace

Her warmth now as ever basks like a flower
Yet this place she has left with her young
Her petals now shine with a love so divine
In a meadow of dazzling sun

My perfect sweet daisy was simply a lady
To my life bringing glorious colour
There forever she'll stay, I'll not pick her away
Always warming my heart like the summer

A few years before I lost my grandmother I had become the proud father of Maggie May. Maggie was my fur child in the form of a miniature Dachshund. She was the apple of my eye, my little shadow and the closest thing I was ever going to have to a baby. On the day I brought her home, she had a chaise-style wicker basket with soft pink blankets and at least a dozen toys. She had a jacket, a T-shirt and a personalised towel for bath time. She was only ever going to get spoiled and she was always going to end up ruling the house. Every morning I would get up and get showered and dressed with an audience – in fact everything I did from that moment on was with a little audience. Often on the weekend Miss M and I would jump in my Z4 and head up to the Gower for an early morning ride. Maggie would sit independently in the passenger seat taking in the fresh air like a vacuum cleaner and when she got tired of that or if it got a little chilly she would ever so gently sneak over onto my lap and cuddle in between my tummy and the steering wheel. Yes, I know there are rules about that kind of thing now, but she loved being there with me and I never had the heart to stop her. Sometimes she would glance up as if to say, 'Is this okay?' Other times she would sneak across and look up as if to say, 'I'm staying here so get used to it.' My reaction was the same either way – I would smile and keep driving. Maggie had such a 'my way or the highway' personality and she was absolutely the princess about the house but I never tried very hard to change her. Movie nights were about a sofa, a quilt and Maggie cwtched up under my chin. If ever J attempted to find room on the same sofa, she would give a very subtle growl and watch him firmly until he had settled on a nearby chair. Maggie wasn't so good at sharing. Everyone loved Maggie, she was the little star of the show and what she lacked in size she made up for with her presence. Maggie was my dog and she became the fur sister to Chester, our Labrador. They were both beautiful and made life so much fuller for the years we had them. Chester died aged thirteen and Maggie died aged six a year later. Maggie had a spinal disease for which ultimately there wasn't a cure. I paid for surgery, but on my second visit to the vets I could see how distressed she was and that she was losing her little battle. I knew there was nothing they could do so I demanded to take her home. She had lost the sparkle in her eyes and was finding it difficult to breathe. I cradled her in my arms for six hours until I eventually gave in and called the vet at 1 a.m.. We drove to the clinic and I walked her in and sat on the floor next to the table they laid her on. By that point she had fallen into a sleepy coma. They injected her little body and I stared right at her in case she opened her eyes. If she awoke, I wanted her to feel safe, to know that I was there. A few seconds before she left me, she did open her eyes and I was right there looking back at her. She looked right at me and licked the end of my nose, and I told her I loved her and she went back to sleep. For weeks afterwards I thought my heart had physically broken and even now I still miss her deeply. I always will. Sleep tight Missy May.

With a Pop And a Fizz

Twinkle toed and fancy free
A silky bear coat to snuggle and shake
Chaotic excitement, the dance of a bee
Joy in abundance and trouble to make

A pink little nose all wet with a wiggle
Charming soft eyes a face oh so sweet
A skip and a hop and a 'look at me' wriggle
Flip floppy ears so pretty and neat

The tiniest heart so full of cuddle
Bright, breezy love always ready to fly
Playful and flirty a plundering muddle
The grass in the meadow the sun in the sky

Under the moon a swift good night kiss
A nuzzle to slumber a sleepy soft yawn
The bundle of treasure has no time to miss
With a pop and a fizz she'll be back with the dawn

2011 came around and with it came the realisation that my relationship of fifteen years was going to end. I was on a downward roll, I had lost my grandmother, cared for and watched J's grandmother lose her battle with a brain tumour, lost my little shadow Maggie May and now the person who had stood by me and held me up though all of that was no longer going to be at my side. It was another full year before we made the final decision to separate known to our families – it took us that long to come to terms with the end of something that we had thought would last forever. We were both old fashioned when it came to sticking with it when the going got tough and we never gave in without a fight, but it takes equal strength to admit when the battle has been lost. It was over and had been for a long time but that was disguised in a deep respect for each other. I guess above all other facts and emotions, we were still there, still waking up next to each other for so long because deep down we still had hope, and hope has a spectacular way of out running reality. Nobody had thrown in the towel under the black cloud of a catastrophic fight, and there was no instant heartbreak, rather a slowly realised sadness that whatever it was we had had for so many years was gone. We couldn't be who we were anymore and we couldn't forgive each other for refusing to accept what (to me) had become the unacceptable option of becoming people we didn't want to be. In a strangely ironic way the death and losses we both experienced in our last few years together served as a kind of lifeline that kept us afloat as a couple, but that lifeline was only ever going to take us so far. So, with love and with respect for the life we'd had together and the potential we both had to still find happiness, we let go. Yet even when you end something respectfully with mutual agreement, you still feel as though you have been stabbed in the heart. It is almost as if the other person already holds the knife in their hand but you were the one who pulled it towards your own chest. I now know that a knife to the heart never truly heals, but the hands of time help keep that a secret, at least.

Once you have loved someone with a depth so great that they have become part of the person you are, part of how you feel and think, they will always stay in your heart. They don't stay there only because you loved them, but also because they also loved you back, and not least because despite the darkness, they helped you build a snowman in the summer.

Today Lost Forever

By the dawn I awoke and forever had gone
In my dream I imagined you reached for my hand
To the night I surrendered our beautiful song
Forgetting our timer was bleeding its sand

The morning brought life, forgetting my loss
In the promise of day I saw only your face
In my world now a void marked with a cross
By my side now a nothing had taken your place

After the noon the rain stared to slow
Not creating a rainbow but a river of grey
I wiped at the current to hinder its flow
Distrusting the sadness not welcome to stay

At night time came calm as I cradled the past
With my heart I still followed you into the night
In my soul laid a truth so hard and so fast
In my freedom of shadows a flicker of light

By my midnight a hope that tomorrow would bring
The triumph of sunrise to show me the way
By myself by my choice be my curse or my win
This today lost forever but I kept yesterday

As the final curtain fell on this colossal chapter of our lives I became deeply reflective. I couldn't help thinking back over the previous fourteen years, about what had been us and the incredible experiences we had been blessed with during our time together. I felt that I had really lived – I mean really lived! There had been so much and all of it spectacular in its own way. I had eaten with Indian tribes on the blood-red rocks overlooking the Grand Canyon, I had rolled the dice in Vegas, prayed with monks in the Xian mountains, walked the Pyramids of Giza, and marvelled at the soul-nourishing views of infinity from the Great Wall of China. I had hailed cabs in New York, ridden carriages in Central Park and stormed dance podiums in Manhattan's west side, Paris, London and LA. I had wined and dined in chateaus, drunk champagne in dinner parties where I was served food that I didn't know what to do with. I had drunk Dom Pérignon and become intoxicated on its vintage while riding on a yacht along Hong Kong harbour (which I might add became the backdrop of my life's worst hangover! Ever!) I'd written poetry and people-watched from a small, monumental garden overlooking the Golden Gate Bridge, stood in the eerie cells of Alcatraz and had fallen head over heels in love with the streets of the Castro, where one of my heroes, Harvey Milk, had changed the world. I'd attended a Papal Audience with Pope John Paul II and wandered the streets of Vatican City before getting lost in the magnificence of Michelangelo's frescos. I'd lounged in jazz bars on Santa Monica Boulevard, mingled in the sordid underworld of Prague, sipped tea in fine tea rooms in Venice, drunk cocktails in Rome, and in dramatic contrast downed lines of shots of all colours and descriptions while semi-naked on foam-soaked dancefloors in Ibiza. I'd been the spectator and the participant in sunrises and sunsets, carnivals and tribal rituals, poverty and extreme abundance, fear and hope, and amongst all of those things I had been awestruck by a thousand fairy-tale vistas. Through most of it I had J right there beside me and in that was the guarantee that what we once had been, would, through memory, always be.

On our last trip to the west coast of the US, I had fancied this snazzy little Diesel jacket that was tempting me every day from a store window on Castro Street. I would stand and ponder it from the sidewalk, unperturbed by the flow of people passing around me. Ultimately the price tag couldn't be justified and so I reluctantly walked away every day, and every day J sighed with relief. On the last night we had drinks and left the hotel to travel to the airport in the privacy of our own limousine. We had hired the chauffeur to end the holiday in comfort, albeit a little earlier than we would have liked, which turned out to be a stroke of luck. The traffic was incredibly busy and I had drunk more of the free sparkling wine that was posing as champagne than I had intended. We had partied all week and when I first lifted the bottle from its ice bucket I could feel J's eyes boring into the back of my head with disbelief as I turned, shrugged and offered, 'Just the one!' So an hour into the journey, I had lost a few inhibitions. We had found the radio and a suitably flamboyant station that was playing disco classics. I was belting out a club masterpiece by Donna Summer, by now swigging out of the bottle, feeling like I was morphing into a combination of Princess Margaret and Patsy Stone! We had left the hotel early and so time was still on our side. In fact, it was perfect, the longer we spent in the car, the less time we had to spend in the always excessively overcrowded SAF. SAF was the code name for San Francisco International Airport – I had completely absorbed airport lingo and code names from J, whose life and work revolved around air travel! On the upside, for fifteen years I hardly ever had to board a plane from a normal departure lounge and instead had a guarantee of access to the executive lounge, where everything was a little more laid-back and a lot more sophisticated. Over the years I got used to the sometimes-stuffy lounges and the often stuffy guests but I always felt a bit fraudulent and expected to be turfed out like a hideaway marched off a boat! No matter how perfectly you dressed in the first-class lounge, or how demure and sophisticated you appeared, you could always spot a fellow faux first-class traveller. They were the ones filling their handbags with miniatures and drinking their way through the cocktail menu like a fish heading into a thirty-day drought. I had once been that fish, but once you realise something is on tap, you tend to stop wanting it! So for us, it was about the peace, relaxation and privacy to read and chat while enjoying a lovely cuppa and the odd single malt!

The traffic was still moving at a crawl. Our limousine had snaked through most of Nob Hill, Downtown and Hayes Valley, heading towards Eureka Valley, and we had come to a stop at a set of lights, which was a prime opportunity to slide the window and get some much-needed air. And there it was, right outside where the limo had stopped, nestled between the streetlight and the sign for the Castro.

Through the neon-edged shop window was my lovely, emerald green Diesel jacket in all its Oz-ified glory. 'Stop the car, I mean hold the car, limousine, whatever it is!' Still holding the wine bottle, I pushed open the irritatingly heavy car door and jumped out. In less than four minutes I was back in my seat, along with the Diesel jacket! Although minus the wine bottle and a few hundred dollars. I had also managed to lose the patience of the driver, who had seemingly lost the charm he had extended when we were first collected! As the limo drove away, I declared, 'Don't say anything, you'll spoil the moment.' Needing to vent his disbelief in some way, J simply placed both hands over his face and shook his head. I knew then and there that there was only so much of me this guy could take in one lifetime 😊.

There was all of that and so much more. There was so much adventure, so much laughter and so many life-changing moments. It had been spectacular, even though I didn't always realise it at the time. And so it goes, je ne regrette rien! Who would? One powerful thing life has taught me is to be present, to be in the moment to use every ounce of energy in your body to see, feel and inhale the people and moments around us. A hundred pretty pictures on a smart phone pale in comparison to the energy in a single moment of happiness. When you chose to be in the moment, that moment survives in your heart and if you've got that then you don't need the photograph. I guess that's why I will never need any photographs of J and I. The moments live inside of me.

Invincible Heart

I needed a change. I needed to do something different with my life and experience a world outside of the one I had created. I felt like I had been through a fire, breathed in too much smoke and now I needed to get out into the fresh air. The Wales that I loved had hosted one too many heartbreaks and as long as I was there, I felt like I wouldn't ever break the cycle. On a Sunday in late November 2012 I packed up two small bags and a suit carrier and took myself to Cardiff Central Train Station. I boarded the 4 p.m. train with a final destination of Brighton. I needed to not only leave my relationship, but my whole life.

That afternoon on the station platform I was desperately trying to bring back my inner warrior who had started to disappear at the hands of my growing fear. My emotions twisted and turned but the fear didn't make way for strength. Instead, I started to slip into a deep anger, a resentful anger that brought tears to my eyes, something the fear had so far failed to do. I was angry with myself, I was angry that I was hurting, I was angry that I was more messed up than I had let anyone know and most of all I was angry that I was terrified. This was my breakout moment, a grasp at independence with greedy hands, and I wanted the movie scene, the big power 'I can do this' ballad blasting out across the station from the announcement speakers. I wanted the moment to silence all the other noise as I waited to board the train.

Instead, I was holding myself together by a thread. A tear had escaped and was tracking downwards across my cheek. I couldn't wipe it away because my hands were full but just as I tried, I was shoved by an arrogant weekly commuter who had absurdly commandeered an exact spot on the platform, a spot that my left foot was clearly not welcome in! My yanked-out earpiece was swinging at my side and there was no power music, just the deafening echo of the bag-dragging groans of people wishing they didn't have to go but knew that they were coming back. In that moment I told myself I was never coming back, and while in retrospect it sounds incredibly overdramatic and even a little clichéd, for the first time I understood what it meant when someone said they needed to find themselves.

I did need to find myself. I had forgotten who I was and one way or another I needed to silence the voices in my head – the crazy ones at least. My reactions and impulses had been learned and my wiring was configured to just get by, to be a spectator at the show (with not such great seats)! Over the years I had stopped listening to my intuition – and I had to own that shit – and I also had to own the processes of shaking that shit off. Despite the disconnect from myself, the little voice of my intuition was still just loud enough for me to hear the call to get outside of my comfort zone and to experience something different. There had to be something more out there, right? I couldn't just settle down with the weight I had acquired. To shift a bag or two shouldn't have been too hard, but I was carrying massive trunks, trunks weighted down with 'stuff' I couldn't even go into without pulling another human being to pieces. It's probably enough to say that some people allow themselves to be walked into the fire, because at first the fire doesn't feel so scary, or hot, but if you keep walking, you'll end up with scars. I had third-degree burns and to a point they were self-inflicted. To a point!

My mother has always said, 'Christopher, you always have and you always will want more. Why can't you ever just be happy?' My mother knows me better than I know myself, and she was right, but this wasn't the time for me to try and break that pattern. This wasn't just about having more; this was about getting back to having enough. I made it to my seat and the train pulled out of Cardiff Central Station. I called my mam to let her know I was on the train and in her warm, loving voice she said, 'Take care, love. I miss you already.' As we approached the Severn Tunnel, the tears flooded my face. I was heading in the opposite direction from the people who loved and cared about me most in this world. I cried on and off for the next hour, feeling as though maybe I wasn't so brave after all. The only tears that fell on that journey were for my parents, who I was going to miss so much, but the tears were balanced with a certainty that I was doing exactly what I was meant to be doing and going exactly where I was meant to be going.

I got to the hotel at around 10 p.m. The Hilton Metropole in all its grandness would be my home for the first six weeks. I ordered a large red (bottle not glass!) from room service and started to run the bath. The room faced the sea, with tall windows that led onto a short terrace. The cold sea wind was blowing and the night had set in and I couldn't see much. I wrestled shut the ridiculously heavy curtains and I hung up my crisp new suit. I called my mum to let her know I had arrived, texted Sazzle, Bette and Jonathan aka Rhoda and waited for the Cabernet Sauvignon in silence. Once room service had left, I sank into the bath and asked my grandmother out loud to pick a song from the hundreds on my phone that would describe the life that was laid out in front of me in Brighton. I took a deep sip from the glass and pressed shuffle. Clearly my grandmother still had a sense of humour – as I drifted off to contemplate the next day and the start of my new life I did so to the soundtrack of Madonna singing 'Girl Gone Wild'! Oh my!

Brighton was my clubbing renaissance. I met a guy in the office called Marc, also from Wales and also gay. A friendship bound for success, as I gravitated to the first Welsh person I met in my bid to escape Wales! Midweek clubbing and meetings with hangovers became the norm. I worked long hours, managing a team of ninety and partied as hard as I worked. A lot! Saturdays became a routine. Gym, shopping for that week's outfit, pre-club drinks at the apartment with friends and a taxi to the club at 10 p.m. to start the night. Sundays became equally as predictable and always started with a two-hour soak in the bath trying to bring my mind and body back to life. I met some great people. What I would call colourful people. The energy of Brighton was addictive and I threw myself into it, and within a few months I was living a completely different life. I had new friends, a full social calendar and loved work. I still missed my folks but I got home as often as I could and, as always, we spoke at least once a day.

Brighton had an almost hypnotic impact on me. I had so much to get out of my system, so much frustration; it was as if a bird had been freed from a cage. I became entangled in the gay community and soon had a large group of friends that were nothing like the friends I had at home. I threw away my inhibitions and went with it. I dated a lot, and occasionally woke up in a random house after an all-night party. I wanted to be that guy that went home before the clock struck midnight but alas I was no Cinderfella! I was having the youth of a single gay man on the addictive gay scene and the drink and the attention was telling me that that I was happy.

The gay world, like all worlds, can be a scary place, and when I first came out I went straight into a fourteen-year relationship, which had kept me in a partial bubble in terms of what gay life had become. Nobody had to go the local gay bar to hook up with someone or to find 'the one' anymore. In fact, I think as far as 'the one' goes, people were over that myth! Apps had taken over. You could start a chat with a guy at 10 p.m., have shared insanely private body pics by 10.05 p.m. and be opening the door to them by 10.30 p.m. to do everything you had committed to doing in the fifteen minutes of chat! For those that don't know, or pretend to not know, you probably think I am exaggerating. I am not! It was easier to get into bed with someone than to order a pizza. It was as though the world had hit reverse – instead of meeting a guy in the bar and buying each other a drink before arranging a date, or even before going home with them, in the new world when you meet a guy in a bar, you have probably already gone way beyond the wink, drink and invitation Now you buy each other a drink to say thank you for what had already been done, or worse, you don't even acknowledge each other, because it was like a business transaction and you are both well and truly over it! It isn't always like that, but it is like that, a lot!

Not everyone was or is like that, and fast love isn't or wasn't for everyone, but I would be a liar if I said that I had been immune to the temptation. What I now know is that sometimes you have to be thankful for the bad shit that could have been worse because without it you could so easily career to that point of no return, the point where you collect a few more scars for the jar! I was a young, single guy living on my own, I was responsible and I was doing nothing to hurt anyone else. I didn't take drugs and I didn't put myself in danger, so I thought. So what harm could it do?

I used the apps all the time, and yes, I had the racy chats, but I had also made friends with decent people, had been on a few really good dates and I had laughed myself out of anything remotely serious as far as sexual invitations went. In all honesty, if you're level-headed it's hard to take it all too seriously. Some guys didn't even speak, their first hello is a photograph of their penis… I mean come on! It is bad enough that you have to speak with too many dickheads on the road to finding a prince, but an actual dick?! Ain't nobody got time for that! However, I could never stop myself from dropping to the pitiful depths of immaturity and responding with my favourite line, 'Don't bring your thing up in here all underdressed and naked, if you liked it then you should have put a ring on it.' That was always followed by a fairly prompt delete, apart from the one time that didn't work because the guy instantly responded with another dick pic, with an actual rainbow-coloured willy ring on it! Credit where credit is due, that was both responsive and impressive. I still deleted him!

It was a Friday night, and for once I wasn't out at the club. I had spent an hour in the bath and had progressed to the sofa, intending to watch TV. Instead I ended absentmindedly scrolling on my phone. I was chatting to this guy and it was heading in the direction I had hoped it wouldn't and any hopes of proper potential had started to vanish. But that was okay, I had no place to be. I was always the sensible one, the guy that didn't throw caution (or dick pics) to the wind in the hope of a sensible response and that worked for me, at least until the night when it didn't. I can't remember the chat or the words that won me over, but that night I agreed against my better judgement to let this guy come over, knowing what his expectations were and having no clue if I was ready or prepared to meet them. I'd said yes, given out my address and mobile number and he had responded quickly to say, 'I am on my way.' It was too late to take it back. Exactly like you would if you were going on a date, I got ready, I sprayed on a tasteful amount of Chanel Bleu, I put on my new Dolce & G T and spent fifteen minutes very carefully creating a hairstyle that looked like it had been mauled by an ape! Fashion, darling! I had used up thirty of the thirty-five minutes I had until ETA. I poured a double Grey Goose to steady the nerves and sat on the sofa in silence. From his pictures he was handsome, not just a little bit, I mean a page turner, and despite the general theme of the chat he sounded really nice, so I kept reminding myself of that, and hey, what harm could this do, right? It was fine, right?

It was just gone 11 p.m. and the intercom sounded. I dashed to the hallway and released the entrance door on the ground floor and then rushed back to the mirror for one last check over. The actual door to the apartment had no spy hole, so I had to wait until he rapped the door with his hand. I practiced my line, 'Hey,' or 'Hi, thanks for coming!' (Really, 'Thanks for coming'? Come on, Anstee!) There was a knock at the door. Fuck, fuck, fuck, here goes! I didn't think that much more about it, I just lunged at the door latch and opened it. He was cute, as good-looking as his photos had suggested, and he was smiling. I stood back to allow him in and said, 'Hey, thanks for coming!'

It was okay at first. We played some music, I made us both three or four drinks, and we talked and laughed about the scene, both having arrived in Brighton from smaller, less flamboyant parts of the country. Half an hour or so had passed and we had started to kiss. Nothing heavy, light touch I guess you could say for want of a better way of describing it. We were lying back on the sofa and we had both properly chilled out with each other. I liked him, but crazy as it may have been I didn't actually *like him*, like him. But he was okay, and great to talk to. We had been messing about for about ten minutes when he started to get a little bit rough, pulling my arm behind my back. He asked me if I liked it. It hurt, and so I was honest and said 'not really,' and started to sit up. He smiled and told me that he liked that, he liked that I was playing with him, that he loved the frigid come on! That was the first, distant alarm bell! I was a little dubious, but not scared – stirred but not shaken, shall we say. I wriggled out from under his arm and off the sofa and had started to stand in readiness to walk away to get us another drink. I'd only put one foot forward when he grabbed the back of my jeans and pulled me back towards him so hard that the leather of my belt had slipped over the top of the jeans and the buckle had dug deep into my stomach. Now I was proper pissed off and said, 'For fuck's sake what are you doing?' His exact words were, 'You fucking love this, don't you.'

I pulled away, not scared but angry, and with all my weight pushed him off, only to be pulled back again, this time with more force, as he grabbed around the back of my neck and pushed my face into the hard arm of the sofa. What the absolute fuck was happening! His hand felt like it was super-sized, like it could have squashed my whole head, and my face hurt from being partially dragged over the harsh beading that covered the armrest. It was lightning fast; in a split second I had gone from laughing to desperately trying to get him off me. His knee was digging in hard on the back of my thighs and he was now partially standing as he pushed his free hand under me to my belt buckle. Only then, in that moment, did the penny drop that I had invited him in, I had agreed to what we would do and he was going to make something happen whether I wanted it to or not. I shouted so loud I thought the roof ceiling would shatter. I was smaller than him, but I forced every joint outwards in every conceivable way, feeling the anger spread to the tips of every part of my body. I had a rush of memory from my childhood when I had been pinned up against the wall outside an English class and forced to endure that idiot's face pressed against mine. It felt the same, that same restrictive pressure that put strength into my body that I didn't think I had. I can only describe it as an eruption as my body forced its way back, upwards and away from him. As fast as it had started, it was over. He stopped – he had got the message. Either that or he had given up.

He stood back and looked at me with disgust and asked what the fuck my problem was. I couldn't believe what he was saying, our discussion had never got near to this kind of shit. It wasn't like the movies when you are shouting at the TV screen as the person in danger is doing and saying all the wrong things, to your utter frustration! I was in the moment and thinking surprisingly clearly. I didn't continue to shout or accuse him of anything, I just said, 'It was good to meet you mate, but you had better go, I am just not into this.' He was silent for a few seconds, and then walked towards me, picking up his jacket off the back of the armchair as he approached, then he kissed me on my cheek, saying, 'No hard feelings buddy, see you around,' and walked to the door! I waited for almost five minutes before I followed behind him to make sure he was gone. I bolted the door, poured myself another drink and turned on the TV. I couldn't concentrate. I was so disappointed with myself, so fucking scared of what might have been and plagued by questions. Was that nothing? Was it really something? Did I ask for that, and what the fuck was I thinking? I went to bed that night, pulled over the duvet cover and thought to myself: get me home.

Vanity Fair

Spin the wheel, start the dance
The decedent, impulsive game of chance
Dress the reflection, paint up the clown
Perfect the attraction, polish the crown

Take the poison, more than you need
Inviting the hunter toying with greed
Face to the flash, you share what's outside
The world now invited along for the ride

The circus pavilion now requires its star
The drumbeat is chasing you into the car
Driven in darkness of calm before form
The final transition, the beautiful storm

The crowd is awaiting the freak show to start
The pathway is calling the dazzling heart
Light hits your face, you're turning the page
Stepping your way up onto the stage

Under the streets with secretive flair
The heroes and monsters of Vanity Fair
Each stranger gets stranger behind the mask
A masquerade ball with a beautiful cast

Demanding approval, commanding the space
Firing the gun, starting the race
The perverted polluted all fade into dark
Only strict invitations to play in this park

The hypnotic bass line, stealing your soul
An orgy of movement, out of control
The poison conspiring to secure your stay
The painting now changing to Dorian Gray

In compulsive delusion, you're clocking the look
Moving in closer, taking the hook
Hard hands take direction, leaving the floor
The frenzied finale, the climax, the score

To the streets in a veil to cover your sight
How garish the day that's stolen the night
The performance is over, you're taking a bow
The curtain is closing; you're on your own now

It was April. I had been in Brighton six months and had just spent the weekend in Wales. I was leaving to head back and thirty minutes into my journey I realised I had left my work bag at my parents' house, so I turned around. I walked in through the front door and my mum was sat on the arm of the sitting room chair, facing the hallway. She was expecting me because I had called to let her know I was on my way back. I looked at my mum. There was brilliant light coming in through the window, shining on my mum almost making it hard to see her face. She was smiling and I smiled back. I grabbed my bag and kissed her goodbye for the second time and left for Brighton. The light and the moment in general played on my mind for a while, but I got on with the journey and parked outside my apartment at around 11 p.m. and hit the sack.

The next day was a free day so I stayed in bed a little later than usual and when I got up just hung around the apartment. It was around midday when the phone rang. It was my mum. I stood in the kitchen, looking out across the lounge and through the windows at the blue sky. It felt like the call lasted only a brief second. I put the phone down after telling my mum everything you should tell a person who has just found a lump in their breast. 'It will be fine, it's probably nothing, just get it checked out to put your mind at rest.' Usually I would have meant all of those things, but this was different. She knew and I knew that this wasn't a 'most of the time' moment. I knew it wasn't good. I started to panic. I paced a bit and then sat down and wished away the next twenty-four hours so that my mum could get to the doctor and prove my instincts wrong. I have forgotten how many times I prayed that day. Not my mum, not now, please.

It only had taken a few weeks to confirm the cancer. After a number of trips back to Wales for consultations, in no time at all we had a full medical diagnosis and a date for surgery. My mum asked me not to come home for the surgery, so I travelled to my brother's home the night before and stayed there in an attempt to disguise my true intentions of being in Wales. When the morning arrived, I drove to pick up my mum and dad, refusing to accept that they would be okay on their own. After the initial round of protest at the fact that I had driven home from Brighton, I could see my dad was grateful for not having to get behind the wheel and I could tell that my mother was happy I was there. That morning we did what we always did, we had a cup of tea, watched a bit of TV and chatted for a short while, but this was nothing like every other day at home. Inwardly, the world was not real. Someone somewhere had pushed autopilot and on we all went. The drive to the hospital was short. Within an hour we had left home, got to the hospital and my mum was in her bed and had changed into her surgery gown. I remember that my mum was in a very practical mood, very matter of fact. I had read a few days earlier that it's easy to be brave when that is the only choice you have, but I disagree. I think it still takes a hell of a lot of strength to put on a steely show when inside you're falling apart with fear. I maintained my fact-based approach, like I had at the other appointments, and likewise gave no sign of weakness. When the time came, my mum climbed into the wheelchair and I pushed her to the theatre with my dad walking behind me. I held the handles so tight my fingers hurt against the plastic ridges. I walked slowly, dreading the moment when I would have to let go. We eventually made it to the entrance door and my dad kissed my mum just as the doctor appeared. I leaned over and kissed her on the cheek, fighting every impulse in my body to cry. Handing over my mum in that chair to the doctor was the most emotionally crippling feeling I have ever experienced. People say that there is no love like the love you feel for a child, but if you're an adult that has never had children, the greatest unconditional love you have felt consistently in your life is the love for your parents. In that moment I was a small boy again on my first day at school, desperate to hold onto her hand. The door closed and my dad and I walked down the long corridor and out of the hospital in silence. I stood in the fresh air and looked at the sky and despite my decision years before to never bargain with God again, I begged God to help us. Inside, I was falling apart, but outwardly someone somewhere else had gifted me with a steely composure that got me through. It was probably my guardian angel. Whoever they were, they worked harder that day than ever before. I couldn't let the weakness out because none of this was about me; it was all about my mother.

Months passed. Treatment started and finished. We went wig shopping and my mum had started to joke about fake boobs and wigs. There was darkness in that time that it brings no value to write about. There was a helplessness that is so hard to describe, but also just when you think you can't love your parents any more than you already do, you have an experience like I had that summer. My mum and dad got through it – smashed their way through it, in fact. I had a whole different level of respect for my mam and all patients that face life threatening or life limiting illness. I saw first-hand how as human beings, people rise up and get taller to diminish the illness, leaving the worry and pain in the wake of their magnificent shadows as they plunge forward, upwards and beyond the reach of their saboteurs. Some don't get that chance to fight, and some don't win the fight no matter how hard they try, but what I saw was that the people who do win don't just win for themselves, they win for their families, their friends and last but never least, for all the spectacular people who just couldn't. They win for life.

I saw strength in my mam that I just hadn't seen before, a gut force that could cut through demons and that elevated my mother to physical and physiological warrior status. When people think of strong women they talk about Michelle Obama, The Queen, Hillary, Oprah. Not now, not in my world. When I think of strong women, or strong human beings come to that, I think of my mother first.

Invincible Heart

Tik tok starts the invincible heart
Another year over to set me apart
A ruthless ambition driving my hand
Creating tomorrow, taking the stand

The rush getting faster, I'm finding my way
I don't recognise life that defined yesterday
The pace now too strong to recover the flow
Many pieces now missing, I start letting go

Time takes my throat like a knife without stopping
By the dazzling sun my heartbeat is dropping
The warning from love comes disguised in a light
A Truth bringing darkness, destroying my sight

In the hungriest sea I am claimed by the tide
My now desperate body so willing to hide
The burden of fear still racing to win
The patience of time unforgiving its sin

The clock doesn't stop to prepare for the start
So I stand in her space, I feel with her heart
By the hand of a moment comes the promise of might
An explosion of strength, an invitation to fight

The night becomes shorter and dawn finds the sun
The love it grows stronger and tempers my run
The beautiful day, a gift now returned
The invincible heart, now humble and learned

Wind changes direction, She's adjusting Her sails
Inspiring life to get back on its rails
Inspiring strength to be all it can be
Inspiring storms to retreat from Her sea

From the shadows there came a gift wrapped up in fire
A ticket to ride my life out on a wire
The blissful awakening, a passion so bold
Empowered by Her, to start breaking the mould

The star of my making, the rocks in my throne
Still teaching me love, still bringing me home
The unconditional heart, the true Mother of nature
I am what I am because love came to save Her

Shadows

Months of sleepless nights, uncertainty and trepidation passed as we lived through all of the many small wins and long pauses of what was to be a long cancer journey. Even when the all-clear came, there were still weeks of adjustment and insecurity lurking in the shadows of our elation, but eventually the fear dissipated, the trust grew, and we were able to focus on the good, the right now and the blessing of the future. We were blessed and thank God my mam recovered. Life was now ebbing back to normality and so I started to cut back on the journeys home to Wales and began to resume my life in Brighton.

I'd been back a while and it took a while to get interested in anything other than the basics, work, friends and making sure everything was okay back home. I had eventually started to date again and had met a sweet guy called Alesandro, I mean being introduced at parties as Christopher & Alesandro had a certain ring to it don't you think? Alesandro was Greek, and can best be described as being the guy off of the CeCe Peniston classic, 'with brown coco skin and curly black hair', oh and he also absolutely had that gentle loving stare, but enough of that! Alesandro was just so funny and cute in every way, including his very continental and somewhat broken English accent. It was our third date and I wasn't sure where it was heading, we hadn't really moved beyond coffee, chatting, laughing and walking but maybe that night it would go one way or the other. We went to my favourite Turkish restaurant on Church Road, and Alesandro looked proper smart. He was wearing a slim grey tweed blazer, a black roll-neck jumper and dark indigo jeans that were hugged by a divine pair of hi shine polished black Vivienne Westwood boots. I mean the fashion for footwear perfection was a mic drop all by itself, I didn't know if I should applaud the triumph or cry for the lack of Viv in my life, I did neither of course and instead stared at them, a lot, with a smile that disguised my glamour boot envy! We talked and giggled and ate and laughed some more and drank some more and it had the beginnings of such a great night. The restaurant was small but warm and colourful and it was always someone's birthday, which usually meant that the staff would surround the celebratory table and sing a Turkish birthday song to a very loud backing track, while the rest of the restaurant would clap along with one hundred per cent investment in the performance. The waiters would sing and dance around to the music as they scurried around the tables and everyone always looked like they were having just the best time. That night was no different but then from nowhere Alesandro's expression became serious and he announced that he had something to tell me. Based on the way he was looking at me, it was either going to be something I really didn't want to hear or something he really didn't think I would want to hear. 'I've got HIV, I've only just started treatment because I refused it for a long time and sometimes I get sick, but I am okay right now and I want you to know.' The waiters still buzzed about singing as they went, the hum of other tables chatting persisted to bustle for position over the music and yet I felt like someone had pressed the pause button. Alesandro excused himself to go to the toilet and I just stared at the table.

I felt devastated that Alesandro was sick and had rejected treatment and I hadn't known him for long but in that split-second I really didn't want him to have HIV, I couldn't bare the pain that I had seen in his eyes when he told me, and if he had continued to reject treatment then surely that would have meant only one thing! A hundred thoughts rushed through my head all at once but in what felt like another split-second Alesandro was back at the table. All I had to do was look into his eyes and just like that all of my thoughts didn't matter, like someone had collected them all up and lifted them away from me. Alesandro looked at me with concerned, sad eyes almost braced and reserved in his posture, 'Are you okay, would you like to leave,' he asked. His face was carrying an expectation of rejection, like he was certain of a negative reaction, and he started to fidget with his wallet, diverting attention downwards to the table. I reached out and took his hand and told him that I was really glad that he felt he could tell me about it, and I asked if he was okay. At first he just shrugged as if to say 'yea but not really.' I let a few short minutes pass and then asked Alesandro what he was thinking. He said that he was sorry, sorry for ruining the evening and sorry for spoiling whatever it was that we had started. I smiled back at Alesandro, 'Nothing is spoiled, you don't have to be sorry, and I am good, we are good and this evening is all good, I mean it would be better if the Viv's were on my feet but meh.' He laughed a little and agreed that 'his' boots were special but they were absolutely 'his' boots and on his feet they would stay! The truth was that I didn't care that he had HIV. I thought I really would care, but I felt absolute certainty right there and then that I really didn't and all I cared about that evening was making damn sure Alesandro knew it!

We talked for hours that night and eventually went back to Alesandro's where we ended up laying on the floor, staring at the ceiling putting the world to rights, while listening to dance tunes and drinking cheap red wine, that actually belonged to his flat mate. He told me raw and powerful stories of how he had coped with the emotional rollercoaster that HIV had become for him and how just having HIV itself had been easier to deal with than the rejection, ignorance and fear that still not only existed but had pushed itself into his life. We shared stories of Wales and Greece from our childhoods and in moments we paused the chatter and just let the music wash over us. Just like the street below, the music had mellowed as time had moved deeper into the early hours and the atmosphere in the room had adjusted to the darkness, with just the streetlights providing a dim glow through the blinds that were hung high on the old sash windows.

'Angels' by the xx had started to play and I turned my head to look at Alesandro who was just in reach to be pulled in for a cuddle. He rested his head on my chest and I pulled him in close and as we both lay there listening to the haunting and yet beautiful, trance like melody of the song; it was a moment I will never forget, because in that single moment I felt more at peace and connected to another human than I had ever felt in my entire life.

Two a.m. became 3 a.m. and 3 turned to 4 and then 5, and it was way past my bedtime and definitely time for me to go. We stood in the doorway to Alesandro's flat, both tired, both still smiling and both staring at each other through sleepy eyes. We had crossed a bridge that night, but nothing physical had happened and I don't think either of us had felt that way. Equally we had bonded at a deeper level and in the romance of the moment, I don't think either of us knew what that now meant. Were we going to walk away or could this be something? I was just about to walk out of the door, but instead in the moment I guess I felt like I had to know and so I turned around and kissed him. It wasn't a particularly romantic kiss, more of a swift plunge and as I pulled away we both looked at each other a little surprised. After a short pause, we started to smile, we both knew instantly, that there was no magic in that kiss, and as I grabbed around Alesandro for a cuddle before I left, he whispered in my ear, 'Let's promise to never try that again!' I laughed and said, 'I promise.' From that moment we spent a few weeks being inseparable, including the night I had to pick his flat door lock with a credit card, and the night he lost his wallet and had to sleep on my sofa and was still there at 4 p.m. the next afternoon watching Disney films, oh and the afternoon I took the bumper off my Z4 because he distracted me and I failed to spot the concrete pillar! In a few short months Alesandro had met someone and we saw less and less of each other but still texted and from time to time we would bump into each other at one of the clubs, and when we did there was always a full on cuddle. Despite never making anything more out of our friendship, we shared one amazing night together and a bond forever cemented in a mutual love for the peace disturbing, art transcending, revolutionary catwalk queen, that is Viv!

I had decided to give dating a wide berth for a while, after one wise

'Bridget Jones' style evening of self-reflection. I had the apartment to myself and so two bottles of rosé in, and to the soundtrack of Gloria Gaynor I decided that I was going to be a powerful independent human being who had no time or place for a man in my busy and important life. The evening made its way from rosé to a couple of whiskies, that ultimately ended in dancing, singing into mirrors and finally a rendition of Shirley Bassey's 'Big Spender', that was performed with a real feather boa and large tube of hairspray cunningly disguised as a microphone! The next morning while nursing my crushing yet short-lived hangover, I accepted the offer of dinner with a chap I had been speaking with online. My abstinence from dating may have only lasted twelve hours, but the break was as good as a rest, as they say! Onwards and upwards.

I had met a few different people but nothing that serious. I had tried New York dating and oh my, oh my, that was just so much hard work. New York dating is when you have multiple dates and you don't commit to any one person until you're sure which one is for you. In theory it works, on a big budget TV show it works, or for people in a big city where you can hide it works, but in Brighton? Not so much. In my reality it was fun while it lasted but it became a bit of a showdown one very normal Sunday afternoon.

And the category is: Shame! Let me share a little about my New

York dating experience. I eventually decided that it was time to give up on the New York dating after a sunny Sunday afternoon out with friends became more than a little tricky. So what is the worst thing that could happen? Easy: exactly what did happen. All three of the people I had been dating all descended upon the same small bar within twenty minutes of each other. When the first one arrived, my mate Karl looked over and said, 'Isn't that the guy you're dating?' 'Yeah,' I said. 'But let's not make ourselves known just yet.' Five minutes later, Karl said, 'Erm... isn't that the other guy you're dating? Wow, awkward.'

Fuck! It wasn't even five minutes after that, I could see Karl was about to speak up again but I got in there first. 'Yes, that is the fucking third and yes I can see that they are all here and yes we need to leave because I am a bad person.'

We made a sharp exit and my days of taking advice from Carrie Bradshaw were over. I should add that 'my' New York dating was mostly undertaken in the old fashioned, romantic sense of the word and was not about sex (at least it didn't have to be). So I spent a lot of my time in restaurants, coffee shops and bars. There was no sex in this city, well not for me at that time anyway, and as far as Sunday afternoon happy hour goes, let's just say for us it was snappy hour. I've never moved so fast! That afternoon I lost a banker, a songwriter and a dance teacher, all in the time it took to take a few sips of a dirty martini!

That afternoon things got cut short, but in reality my drinking was getting worse. While I was never close to being an alcoholic, I knew I was out too much, drinking too much and generally heading in an uncharted direction. I wasn't myself anymore. I would let the smallest things take up all my thoughts, I had become a pathological overthinker and there were moments where I had to remove myself from people to consider the hundreds of voices that had started to play over and over in my head. I was starting to wonder if I needed a check-up from the neck up, but how does anyone know when it's time to speak to someone, when it's time to say: 'I am not well here, I need help!' I don't think we do know, so we just keep going, feeding the demons to leverage a few moments of weightlessness, a few moments when we either feel okay or can pull off feeling okay.

I was always ignorant when it came to psychological disorders. I always thought that I was one of the people in this world that could shrug anything off with a stiff upper lip. I never really understood or identified with what I thought of as the other kind of people that life could bring down to the extent that they got ill. In retrospect, that feels like such an immensely insensitive outlook now that I know better. It wasn't that I ever disbelieved or doubted the suffering, I guess I just always thought that would be someone else, not me! I unconsciously segregated people into two different groups and I put myself in the strong one. How wrong I was. After weeks and months of ignoring the symptoms I woke up one morning after a very short sleep and looked in the mirror at my grey, exhausted reflection. I didn't recognise myself. I was one of the other kinds of people and I had no idea how I had slipped into that group. I had become obsessed by my own mortality and health, and at any given moment, but much more frequently at night, I had a voice in my head steering me to another illness that I might have. From the moment that voice was allowed to speak I would surrender all practical, rational control of my behaviour. I would feel overwhelmed by the need to check my body and no conversation, interaction or life scenario had the ability to silence that voice until I had checked myself during episodes that could last from twenty minutes to three hours. I would leave dinner tables at restaurants and hide in the toilets, I would take myself from bed in the middle of the night or abandon movies and social gatherings. I knew it was escalating, and I felt like I was starting to lose myself. As the voices got stronger, my resolve got weaker and weaker.

I was mentally and physically exhausted from another tormented night of torment. The actual process I would go through was horrific. I would check my body from head to toe, sometimes over and over until I had no energy left. That previous night I had stood, freezing cold, naked, in the bathroom. Behind the locked bathroom door, I searched my whole body for lumps, terrified that I would come across something that would tell me I was ill or that I might die from cancer. At the time there was no reasoning with the compulsion, and no concept of the fact that it was 4 a.m. and you have already been there for hours. There is no awareness that your body temperature has dropped and that you are actually freezing cold. The only thing you can think about is getting to the end without finding the one thing that would turn you into a 'Dead Man Walking'.

Some days I would have to hide parts of my body that had become inflamed and bruised from the excessive poking and prodding. I would have to cut short things I had planned to do or delay and cancel appointments. I wasn't depressed – I was terrified. Terrified of becoming ill and what that feared illness would do to the people around me. From a place of selflessness, I had become inexplicably self-absorbed in my own death.

Eventually, I felt utterly defeated and lost. I spoke to a doctor and within days I was receiving help from a counsellor and although at the time I had convinced myself that it wouldn't work, I now class myself as one of the lucky ones, because the demons that the counsellor forced me to face soon started to disappear. The sessions were tough and the soul searching was often painful, but there was something about the environment that meant that you spoke from a place of pure truth. This stranger, this non-judgemental human being through gentle questioning had allowed me to see my truth, my pain and my insecurities, but much more positive than that, they showed me the root cause of my problems and ultimately the power to change my wellbeing.

I used to go to a small, converted shop space to meet Hilary, my counsellor. It was a non-descript, dull building and the room itself was on the second floor at the very back, which meant you had to go through a warren of grim hallways and staircases to get there. The room was very simple, furnished almost as though it was still the 70s, with its veneer-covered tables and retro artwork. The old tan leather chairs retained their leathery smell and they dominated the room with their rigid tall backs and elegantly studded, worn arms. There were a few pot plants scattered across the windowsill and a huge arched window that overlooked some trees and a scrappy, uncared-for garden that had been overrun by almost Jurassic weeds. The room was so bright; sunlight flooded through the glass and brought with it some warmth from the early morning sun. When the weekly session had arrived and I eventually made my way across town and through the chaos of traffic and the thousands of lives milling past me, I would take off my coat, sink into that chair and give in to a feeling of pure, unadulterated peace. I started to enjoy the experience: like offloading ugly, heavy baggage that had weighed you down even though you had no idea it had been there. We spoke about sex, drink, death, loss, love and everything in-between and while I was often taken aback or moved, I never felt moved to tears. It was only in one of my last sessions that I finally broke down and let the floodgates burst. When I say burst, I *mean* burst, the kind of crying that leaves you with that sobbing, breath-catching shudder for at least twenty minutes after you have stopped. The kind of crying where you need a recovery room and a few paracetamol to shift the headache that your face strain has brought on. I had been asked that one question that in answering you admit your deepest vulnerability, your neediness, your disappointment, your sadness and your desperation to be loved. In that moment you are transported back to being a little boy, lost, alone and desperately searching for the protection and love that you have only ever known from your mam and dad. That's how I felt. I wanted my parents, I needed them, but they had been through too much for me to add to their worries. I cried so hard both for the moment of realisation and for what they meant to me. There was an acceptance of pain that I had both created and subjected myself to that had stolen my capacity to stay strong. There was the realisation that I had carried too much by myself for too long and then there was the greatest realisation of all: that my spirit, my confidence, my potential and my life all deserved much more than I had allowed it to settle for.

The mountain felt so high and impossible to climb in the beginning, but I got through it and I made it to the top where I had the most powerful retrospective view of my life and a clear view of the journey that had brought me to that place.

I didn't need any medication and nor did I want it. I never had time away from work and I called upon my stubborn determination to get back to normal no matter how hard the journey seemed. I listened, I read, I did the exercises, I meditated and I fought those mother-fucking demons with every ounce of my being.

What I had developed was a chronic case of Health Anxiety Syndrome (HAS). It was the obvious manifestation of years' worth of exposure to an unhealthy relationship, declining self-esteem and fear bred from the loss and near loss of those I loved most in this world. I have so much respect now for those that suffer from any form of psychological anxiety or disorder and a patience and tolerance that didn't exist in me before. I was a fool to dismiss it as something other, weaker people suffered from and I was ashamed that I ever thought that. I now know that it is something the strongest people can get. It is not a sign of weakness but a sign of life, a sign that someone has been too strong. It is not a sign of lower intelligence, but a sign of a depth of thought and analysis that has breached the boundaries of what a human can cope with. It is not something to shy away from or sweep under the rug. Nor is it something to be ashamed of, but rather it's something to tell people about, so that everyone who lives it and feels that isolation today can know that every new moment brings the potential to start a magnificent recovery. I only feel that my life briefly dipped into stormy waters and so with the greatest respect for those that are drowning I won't pretend that I can ever understand the level of torment or suffering that brings. I never wanted to take my life, I just didn't want the version of it I was living.

Staircase

Life down a staircase, out through the door
Stop the clock ticking; take my feet off the floor

Inviting a distance, dismissing false light
Chasing the darkness, creating my night

Drowning in safety, cradled in still
Smothered by fears, breathing at will

Chaos moves faster, slower moves time
Demons creep closer, crossing my line

Cold blood rushes through me, I cripple with hate
Muscles like statues, defining my state

Shutting my eyes, not to look, but I see
My tormentor crawls closer, to suffocate me

Curled up in disguise, a tear leaves its place
Deceiving its maker, betraying my face

A screaming surrender, a grovelling cry
From the pits of despair, in this blackness I lie

My mind now disfigured, I'm losing all trace
Taken by hatred, by his hideous grace

I feel but a spirit, it scratches my heart
Frozen like ice, I start chasing the start

Effortless hope, I fold from the floor
The feather is falling; this war is no more

Seeing the staircase, my pulse starts to slow
Reaching for freedom, warm blood starts to flow

Pushing the window, touching the sky
Now sitting, now breathing, now willing to fly

Love on the breeze, breath on my skin
A sparkle of brilliance, letting life in

Brightness responding, a wishing to be
My feet on the floor, now carrying me

One stair on the staircase soon turns into four
The shadow that's watching will be back for more

From the weight that I carry, from the bundle I hide
Comes the heart that destroying, the thorn in my side

I was in rebuild mode, and I was confident again. As time passed, I was becoming more fearless and I started to like the reflection in the mirror more and more every day. It was early summer and there was lots of anticipation for the upcoming Pride. Pride was one thing I had always wanted to do and had never had the chance. I couldn't think of any better way to pay tribute to my freedom-fighting heroes and to kick to the curb any residual insecurity I had about being me, feather boas and all! There was already a buzz about Pride in general that year and it had just been announced that the theme was to be Icons, in a bid to bring about a lavish celebration that emphasised the massive array of LGBTQ allies, campaigners and celebrities that had shaped LGBTQ culture. A few friends had asked me to do it and I was so ready. Plus, let's be honest – it was never going to be difficult for me to pick an icon to pay tribute to, now was it! So on August the 7th 2013, at 10 a.m. I stepped out of my mate's apartment in a huge white tutu, a boy toy belt and as many crucifixes as I could lay my hands on. It was already blisteringly hot and I was wearing a vogue-esque top hat with matching feather boa that soared a metre into the sky before cascading back over my shoulders and down my back. My custom T-shirt read, 'L.U.V Madonna' on the front and on the back was 'H.R.H Anstee of Hove Actually'! I looked ridiculous and yet it was fabulous and I had absolutely no inhibitions at all. When I crossed that seafront road I was feeling prouder than I have ever felt, because I was proud of myself, the storm I had recently dragged myself through, and the sense of self that I had reclaimed. I didn't stop the traffic I wanted to stop, crossing the main road that morning, because let's face it this was Brighton on Pride Day, no shocks to be had in this town. My outfit was practically pedestrian in comparison to the glamazons we were about to witness. We had to wait for an hour before the parade started, and the excitement was building minute on minute as all of those marching lined up out of sight, desperate to get this extravaganza on the road.

At 11 a.m. sharp we started to move and soon after our group hit the main route. 'Radio Ga Ga' was blasting out across the streets and confetti flares fired off in all directions. The crowd was solid, at least ten people deep at most sections of the route, all cheering, all clapping, all going crazy with support and pure love and respect. There were babies and kids and grandparents. It was the most beautiful thing I had ever experienced; the feeling of pride was overwhelming, and I shed tears on many occasions during that march. A sea of banners in every colour of the iconic rainbow waved, all emblazoned with messages of peace and love and freedom. There were quotes from one of my heroes, Harvey Milk, floating on fabric from an office window on North Street and balloons escaping up into the air everywhere I looked. There were party floats, showgirls, show boys, drag queens, dance troops, trans representation, and AIDS and HIV representation, and amongst those of us celebrating our equality and freedoms were small groups of our wider world community representing the struggles and fight of our still-oppressed brothers and sisters. People raced swiftly from the barriers to get photographed with us as others shouted out words of love and support. The heat disappeared and the sense of occasion engulfed us all. I felt an overwhelming sense of belonging and brotherhood/sisterhood, as though we could march through anything and change the world. I will forever remember that march: how the people, the music and the atmosphere elevated us all to a place we had never been before. I will never forget how it made me feel.

Along the way I saw work colleagues, new friends, some not so new friends and many memorable faces beaming with joy just to be spectating. As the march moved to its final post, I clocked my best friends who had travelled from Wales to see me. They looked so happy to be there, and I was so happy to see them stood there waving back. And just like that, one of life's rare moments of pure, unadulterated happiness. We crossed the finish line and like those before us and after us we screamed and cheered with everything we had, just to make sure the whole of Brighton could hear us. As the late, great Harvey Milk said, 'Hope will never be silent.'

Pride is such a powerful state when it is truly experienced and I was proud with every inch of my being on that day. We go on a journey to live our lives, we come out not just once but over and over again, we come out every time we make new friends, visit old relatives, start new jobs and we keep coming out because living out loud is the only way to redefine society, to overpower the fear in others and to make the way for those that come behind us. We face bullies, people who think we are less than them, people who think we deserve to die because we simply want to live, and we sometimes lose people we adore, because they are not ready for our truth. Some of us are disowned, orphaned by the people who made us feel the safest in the world. As a community we live a million different experiences and some are fantastic, and some are life limiting but by majority we take it all in our stride, we make it look easy, like it is really no big deal, and yet most of us go through it. We fight to be ourselves despite the haters, fight to live out loud out of respect for the kids who think suicide is easier than facing the truth and we fight to be included and equal. We are warriors who had to persuade the world to accept us and until every kid choses life and truth, pride in all its life changing power needs to be enforced, shared and celebrated in spectacular fashion.

Half A Crown

Pride had come and gone and I had started to knuckle down at work and I stopped going out as much as I had been. I was back at the gym every day, I was running and making plans to sell my small but beautifully formed chapel conversion in Wales, in a bid to free myself from financial limitations. Buying the chapel had turned out to be a great move for me. It had been my first strike at independence after my relationship with J had ended and it was another rope that anchored my life to my roots, my home town and my family. I had fallen in love with it and part of its charm was that it overlooked the town cenotaph, and the first name on that cenotaph was Fred Anstee, my great uncle. It may sound a little strange that a cenotaph could bring charm to a house but it did to me and it bonded me to the place. It wasn't just that Fred's name had been on it, but it was the story that my dad had told me about the young and gentle-natured Fred Anstee that had always captured my attention.

Fred was only twenty-one years old when he had to go to war. My father was only a small baby, the first-born son to my grandfather, Fred's brother. The night before Fred left, he visited my grandparents to see them, but mainly to see my dad, his baby nephew. He placed half a crown in my dad's little hand before saying goodbye and even now when my dad tells me the story of Fred's brief visit and the half a crown, his eyes light up with warmth and pride. Fred had his whole life in front of him, just like thousands of other young men and women, but when the day arrived, he put on his uniform and boarded the lorry that would take him away from everything he knew and loved. The lorry that would take him away to fight for his home, his family, his country and for the future of his little baby nephew. He would fight so that younger generations wouldn't have to.

It was only days, not even weeks, when the news came that Fred had died in action, killed by German bombers before even leaving English soil. There was no grand flag-draped coffin delivered by army officials back then, as there were just too many to send home. Family friends had to travel to bring back his broken young body to be buried as a hero by his grief-stricken parents, brothers and sisters.

When the cenotaph in Porth was first erected Fred's name wasn't there. My father made it his mission in his adult life to honour his uncle's memory and to make damn sure that Fred's name was put on that list of lost men and women. Eventually his details were found and matched with the national records and his name was placed at the very top of the list in silver letters engraved forever against the black marble that stood just outside what would become my front door. My dad was too young to remember Fred Anstee on the night he placed that half a crown into his small hand, but he never forgot who he was and neither will I.

I was blessed to have grandparents and parents who shared endless stories of the war, stories that were sometimes painful, but equally sometimes warm, humorous and heartfelt. Either way, the stories were always captivating and because of them and because of Fred Anstee I was blessed with opportunity to develop an unfaltering respect for the soldiers who battled for our peace, the true freedom fighters of their time. Those soldiers were not just fighting to save the world from dictatorship, but for all manner of freedoms and futures. Hitler wanted to take over the world, to deliver a master race in the image of what he saw as perfection. There is a saying, 'Don't let perfection become the evil of good.' I guess that couldn't be more true in this case. So we didn't just win a war, we won the right to have a future, whatever our background, race, sexual orientation or political view. That war was in my view the biggest fight for equality and tolerance the world has ever fought and therefore should never be forgotten or taken for granted.

I sometimes worry that memories of them will fade. I don't like to think so because Fred Anstee was one of my own and the thousands of men and women all around the world that died all belonged to someone. So I have made a vow that I will keep telling Fred's story, and any story I remember from what I know, to keep a respect alive that should never die with them, or us, the keepers of their memory. The truth of the matter is that yesterday's battles for freedom show us how to fight the next, and without them we wouldn't be able to enjoy the freedom we believe in today. Without Fred and all the others like him, thousands of us may never have been able to be who we are now free to be. God bless you, Fred Anstee.

As I made plans to sell the chapel, I knew I was growing tired of

Brighton. I had toyed with the idea of going back home. I spent less time with new friends and gravitated towards my besties, who I persuaded to visit me whenever they could. My company had recently acquired a new business in Essex and I had discussed the potential of working from that location with my director, but it was just an option and not one that I was sure about back then. Just as I had craved the change and adventure of leaving Wales, at that point I was starting to feel the tug of heart strings calling me back home… that is until someone else decided to fiddle with them!

No Day But Today

It was April 2014 and I had just met someone online (well I met someone online most days, but this was one of the one in ten who were worth having more than one conversation with). Despite the narrow odds and having dodged a few more frogs with dick pics, I finally had met someone who had not only managed to survive a whole two weeks, but who had even been promoted to WhatsApp! This wasn't just rare – it was unheard of! It was a case of so far so good – his replies were intelligent, he could make me laugh, and had no obvious serial killer-style tendencies.

As it turned out – somehow – this guy worked for the company that we had acquired and was based in Essex where I had travelled to on a number of occasions. What were the chances? He could have been a butcher from Glasgow, but no, he was in IT and worked in my office! The upside of this discovery was brilliant, although what wasn't so hot was the thought that we had maybe passed each other in the office a hundred times and not even noticed each other! I had started to travel to Witham, Essex as part of a cultural transition and I had a meeting booked for 10 a.m. on a Wednesday morning. We had agreed to meet on the corner outside the office at 9.30 to go for coffee but my journey had not delivered me in the state that someone would like to be in for a first mini date.

I had been up since 5 a.m., taken three trains and a tube across London (lugging two large bags and a laptop the entire way), I had tripped, dropped my suit jacket and almost landed on the tracks while running for a connecting train and, worst of all, had failed to secure my coffee intake, instead settling for a tea that I had managed to spill on my trousers when trying to fit the flimsy, flappy, floppy lid onto the takeaway cup while strutting to my carriage. I felt like I had been through an assault course and lost. I wanted to look all Bradley Cooper (yes a stretch I know) but instead walked all the way from the station to the office looking like Edina Monsoon on crack!

I could see him stood on the corner outside the office waiting for me, so I swiftly tried to create as much composure in my appearance as was possible while moving with both hands full and a jacket that was by this time sliding down my arm and threatening to drop to the ground at any point. He on the other hand was as well turned out as I expected him to be and in fact even cuter than I thought, which is always a bonus. We walked to a Costa Coffee and sat there for twenty-five minutes having the polite chit-chat you would expect while I mentally tried to prepare for my presentation. I thought he was very easy on the eye and a generally nice bloke, I didn't think too much more about it at that time, but it was good to meet him. We exchanged a few more texts but nothing major and a few weeks passed before we realised that we were both at the same management session in London together, so we agreed to meet for mini date number two. That night was so much more relaxed; we talked all night without a single awkward silence. He was funny and had a nice energy about him and he didn't do anything or say anything to put me off, which was normally the case.

It was on the train back home that I decided to ask him to come to Brighton that weekend. He very swiftly replied with a yes, which was of course the right answer. I can't remember the exact date but it was the week after Eurovision and Conchita Wurst had won the title, I don't even remember the song, but I will always remember Conchita. Real name Thomas, he didn't really go on to live up to his groundbreaking performance on Eurovision and sadly rejected his platform to be a spokesperson for HIV, only coming out about his positive status after being blackmailed. Of course, that was his absolute prerogative, but it seemed sad that he felt he couldn't do that and be that person. Anyway, we digress, again!

So it was Brighton weekend and our first full on proper date, and if it fell flat it would be torture because he kind of needed to spend the night, having driven all the way from Essex! He arrived late, to a house full of my mates watching YouTube clips of Eurovision while getting more and more drunk by the second. After a swift costume change and a round of introductions we all hit the town for the normal Saturday night out with the gang – well as normal as it could be while kind of having date number three with an audience. My mates loved him, I mean really, at one point I almost had to fight to get a word in. The night sashayed into a mist as they always did and before we knew it we were in our taxis home to bed. In the morning the sun was blazing and so we drove up the coast for breakfast and a walk across Hove beach. I remember parking my car and him telling me not to leave my soft top open. I explained that I always left the roof off my car in good weather and that it was safe in Hove actually. He turned to me and said, 'No, put it up, you're not leaving it like that.'

Not normally very good at taking commands I surprised myself by swiftly hitting the button to close the roof. I smirked to myself as we got out of the car, thinking: *How rude, so masterful – I must like this one*!

It had all gone so well but before we knew it, the morning had disappeared and it was time for him to go back to Essex. I can't describe what it was that I was feeling. It certainly wasn't love, but when he left I felt like I had lost a little limb! What the hell was that all about! So it had happened, for the first time in a very long time someone had got under my skin. His name was Mr H, by the way, not 'he'!

The next weekend was a bank holiday and so we spent another weekend in Brighton blessed with hot sunny days and clear blue skies. That weekend we discovered we had a shared respect for Christina Bianco and Bagpuss, the fat, furry cat-puss, and it felt like we spent the whole weekend laughing and trying our best to outdo each other attempting to recreate the Bagpuss opening monologue. We drove around town and down the beautiful East Sussex coast to Burling Gap, where we stopped for a while and walked to the cliff edge before heading down to the small coffee shop at the beach. Mr H's one-night stay turned into two and in the moments we weren't walking, driving and laughing, we were eating – something we were both very good at.

There are a variety of dating stages. The first is the 'I think you're okay but I'm not sure I like you yet' and often that kills the need for the second stage. The second is 'I like you but you could still be a serial killer, so I need more time'. The third is the nice stage; this was the stage we were at that weekend. The 'getting to know you because I already know I like you and you might just be a keeper' stage. On the Monday morning I sat at my desk with a big smile. The PA that sat to my right was all over it. She knew about the one-night stopover in Brighton and the first thing she said was, 'Oh my God, look at you, I knew it, he stayed the whole weekend didn't he?'

She was right, of course.

Christina Bianco was a female voice impressionist we both loved, a very clever and very funny one at that. I had heard of her briefly before but having watched her live concert clips on YouTube that weekend I was a little hooked. When Mr H left to go back to Essex I looked her up online. Not only was she on a world tour, she was in Brighton that Wednesday! I didn't call to check, I just booked the tickets and sent Mr H a text at work on the Monday morning. At worst he would wish he could have made it, at best he'd come back to go with me. Two days later, Mr H was back.

We got to the venue late and so we had to grab a few chairs near the bar. The show was amazing. It was midway through and the song 'No Day Like Today' started. It was a song made famous by the musical *Rent* and I had loved it since I first heard it many years before. The song was being performed by a drag queen who was singing during interludes and he was doing such an amazing job. I wanted to grab Mr H's hand but I wasn't sure he wanted me to, but just as I had settled my hand firmly back in my lap he beat me to it and reached over to take my hand. Christina had come back out of her dressing room. She was standing to the side of us and gave us a big, warm smile. She was tiny and very beautiful. And it was only holding hands, a song, and a C-list celebrity smiling at us, but in that moment, I knew I had fallen in love just a little bit. After that I was done for and so the romance started for the three of us: Mr H, Bagpuss and I. Bagpuss had become our little mascot and so it was essential to purchase a pint size Bagpuss in recognition of that fact! He was given his own Facebook account and we found taking photos of Bagpuss in strange places highly amusing. At the peak of his fame our Bagpuss would often receive in the region of a thousand hits. One of his all-time greats was his photograph in the 'I'm In Miami Bitch T-Shirt' (taken during our trip to Miami, strangely enough). Other famous moments included his appearances at the Shard in London and at Grand Central Station in New York. The biggest crowd puller was the controversial picture of Bagpuss with the kissing policemen by Banksy, which received a whopping two thousand hits from all over the world. Alas, the fame didn't last for long and Bagpuss entered early retirement in January 2015. Mr H and I, however, went on as a duo.

Within four months we had been to Miami, Orlando and Key West together and had booked our tickets to spend our first Christmas together in New York, which turned out to be as special as we had hoped. In some ways we were a terrible combination – impulsive, frivolous, with a 'what the hell' attitude. We both liked our own way and neither liked to be told. I thought he was a princess and he called me a princess! He drove me stir crazy and I know I had a similar impact on him. He challenged me and said 'no' a lot, which was not something I had ever been used to having to deal with, so I guess I had all the evidence to suggest that I may have met my match. One thing is for sure, on paper Mr H and I probably shouldn't have worked, but sometimes the world conspires to create something, be it for a season, a reason or a lifetime and that is definitely what happened with us.

Before we knew it, we were settled, and we had established an almost perfect life in a quaint village on the Suffolk boarder. The village was beautiful, with a flurry of thatched cottages, an old church that looked over the village from the top of the hill and a small, rickety pub bursting with old country charm. The village was surrounded by vast open fields and a few nearby fishing lakes that were all within walking distance from our place. Before very long I was immersed in village life and I had been welcomed by everyone including some of Mr H's oldest friends. Friday nights consisted of venturing down to the pub to join what had become our small, friendly crowd, while lazy Sunday afternoons were normally spent around Mr H's mum and dad's house, which was also in the village. We would sit there for hours watching TV while we waited for the amazing Sunday roast to arrive amongst never-ending servings of tea. You only had to put a foot in the door and there was a cup on its way! It's not essential to like your other half's folks, but I did, I liked them a lot. The village and my life were so very different to my time in Brighton, in fact the city had started to feel cold, busy and distant. The village had become my breath of fresh air, literally. The North Essex countryside was stunning and I was living right in the middle of it.

A few years passed, and what can I say? I was in my late thirties and yet only on my second 'serious' long-term relationship. Things weren't as perfect as I had hoped, but then life had changed me and I had long since realised that life and people were never as perfect as we might wish them to be – and I include myself in that little nugget of wisdom. Mr H and I were different, and these differences became more challenging as the months passed and we both became less able to tolerate what didn't work in the relationship. Although I had left my dark days behind, with every new chapter there are new and different patches of shade that we pass through. I guess what I am saying is that things got tough, the honeymoon period ended faster than I would have liked and I feel as though our relationship aged beyond its years. What I will say for Mr H and I is that because of our ambitious 'get things done' attitude, we always got what we wanted as a couple.

We made things happen, I don't know how, but if we wished for something we made it come to life. We may not have always been the most sensible of couples but what others sat around thinking about we went out and did. 2015 became a strange year and there were highs and big lows and we had a few opportunities to test our resolve and the depth of our feelings. But then as 2015 moved into 2016 we were still together. I had learned to persevere, to give things a chance, to make things work. With J I had done that too much for too long, but this felt right, it felt like we had something worth having, something worth holding onto. We had developed such an intense relationship at the start that our staying power turned out to be linked to the realisation that we had to almost grow apart in order to stay together. We were always both fiercely independent and we needed to find that balance where we existed both as partners and people in our own right.

Little Leaf

You are a mystery to me
Like the leaves that resist the wind through the tree
Like the tree that holds tight to its autumn leaf coat
While the storm's hands are clasped around its weakening throat

In our glorious spring we slept through the sun
In the autumn we woke to the sound of a gun
A summertime lost in a dream that has drifted
A wishing for strength in a winter soon lifted

The dusk is no threat to the light of a fire
The dawn is a promise that night will surrender
Surrender its shadows that threaten the light
Restoring its brilliance, disarming the fight

I'm not letting go; said the leaf to the tree
I will never survive if your hands set me free
I will never feel warmth from your heart or the sun
So if I do fall away then my heart will not come

The winter is tomorrow and for now you're with me
This autumn we have still has so much to be
Little leaf you were born to be cradled by light
To withstand the wind and to dance through the night

Today is our time so let the morning take flight
No wind or a winter is nearing sight
A story to make and a sky to inspire
Like a leaf to its tree this love will not tire

Je Ne Regrette Rien

It felt like it was only yesterday I was loading perfectly clean clothes into a cardboard washing machine on my fifth birthday, blissfully content with life, without a single trouble in the world. Somehow, in the blink of an eye, I had travelled the long and winding yellow brick road to forty and crossed more than a few bridges over troubled waters during the journey. I had met a few cowardly lions, a few men that had no hearts and come to think of it a few that were all straw and no brain. I have conversed and contended with the odd witch and I even had my own Toto. You can see where I am trying to go with this right? No? Okay, so maybe my life is a contemporary take on *The Wizard of Oz* and I am in fact a man-Dorothy. I even like blue gingham, although I draw the line at ankle socks. There is one item that I would never refuse to have in my closet and that would be a pair of sparkly, ruby-red size ten heels. Not just because they are iconic, pretty and fairly fabulous, but for a man who has spent so much time away from home, I would have given anything on many occasions to have just been able to tap those bad boys three times to then appear back in Wales. There is no place like home, after all. One thing is definitely true: I have still not reached my metaphorical Emerald City.

I was thirty-nine and even if the yellow brick road was still stretching out ahead of me, and Emerald City not in sight, I did feel like I had made it to a review point, almost as if I were midway up a tall mountain. As I turned back to look at the path I had taken, I could recognise every last event in my life and the reason it had to happen. I recognised and was grateful for every lesson I had learned and the pain I had endured at times, all of which had helped to make me who I had become. I owned it all, and I wouldn't have changed anything. Je ne regrette rien. The beautiful thing was the older I got the higher the vantage point I stood at became, like the landscape below was stretching and twisting into glimmers of wisdom and self-worth. I had aged but I was still young, and some are not blessed with that opportunity. I was wiser and I knew an awful lot more about who I was and what I wanted out of life.

It appears that we really only start to know what it's all about once we have started to lose our hair, gain a few wrinkles and put a few miles on our body clocks! Maybe that's all part of it, maybe as we get older we are meant to start dismissing the meaningless vanity of life to expand our vision into seeing what is really important. Someone once asked Bernard Shaw what, in his opinion, is the most beautiful thing in this world. 'Youth,' he replied, 'is the most beautiful thing in this world – and what a pity that it has to be wasted on the young.' That answer always makes me smile but my view is that youth is our training ground, our adult childhood and the frivolous party we have to attend on the bridge between being a kid and a mature human being. I think the idea is not to party too hard on that bridge so that you are still in one piece when you get to the other side. No matter what side of the bridge you are on I am equally convinced that you have to keep moving forward and owning everything you have come from without turning back to look at it. A fool trips up on the past but a wise man trips up on the future while trying to find his way.

So when I turned forty, I was determined to not stand still on the vantage point of my metaphorical mountain of life for long. But then I thought what harm could it do to have a party before setting back off on the yellow brick road to find the bloody Wizard. For years I had toyed with the idea of big expensive trips abroad and all other kinds of celebration ideas for my fortieth birthday but in the spring of 2015 I settled on the idea of a black tie party. It had to be in Cardiff, and it had to be special and so I embarked on planning what I eventually titled La Soirée Noire, or in English, The Black Evening. Titled as a reflection of the colour scheme, not because I was mourning the passing of my thirty-something status or youth in general.

I had often wondered what my fantasy party would look like, or a fantasy dinner party at least. If I could have an evening in the company of any group of people irrelevant of their mortal state, then it wouldn't be in the presence of celebrity but of family that I had and had lost or had never had the privilege of meeting. That would be my truest fantasy dinner party, in fact with that company I would be happy with a cup of tea and a few biscuits around an open fire, no dinner required. I am not sure I would even need to speak, just being there with those people would be enough, even it was for just a few short minutes.

But if I had to draw up a guest list for a fantasy dinner party based on worldly celebrated people that I feel have been icons to me in my life? If some twisted, elegant dimension opened its doors to me and that party became part of the art of the possible, then I guess it would have to look something like this:

My Fantasy Dinner Party – Dream Sequence

The grandfather clock strikes 8 and the loud echo of the doorbell is synchronised with the clock's final chime, announcing the arrival of my first guest. I glance hard in the mirror and make a final adjustment to the deep grey and white polka dot bow tie that I have chosen, just for this occasion. In my reflection I see the first lines of age starting to appear, the first signs that I have lived, perhaps, and the first signs that I had experienced enough life to have something worthwhile to say about it. Let's hope so. The room around my reflection is dark, and I can barely see the pattern of the grey floral wallpaper that is reaching up towards the high ceiling and the dimmed chandelier that is hanging over its opulent kingdom. The room is vast but still, with the exception of the heavy velvet curtains that shift gently with the wind that passes through the French doors, which are open just enough to hear the music coming from the terrace below. The teasing tones of 'Tiptoe Through the Tulips' by Tiny Tim flow with an eerie, broken crackle, as if being played on a very old gramophone.

I push myself away from the dressing table and walk to the bedroom door to listen, to find out if I can hear the voice of my first guest. At first nothing but then something. I can, I can hear it, and I smile with pure disbelief and awe as I detect what can only be the charming, clever and unmistakable tones of Oscar Wilde. I turn and rest my back against the door in a swift, playful and – dare I say – almost camp motion, so tempted to twist the doorknob and wander out onto the landing to take my first peek at this legend of a human being. Instead, I smile and hold in the anticipation, enjoying its power just like a child on Christmas Eve. Anticipation becomes all the more inviting when you get closer to the moment. Time starts to lose its wicked power and you start to gain control in the smug knowledge that time's time is running out.

I pace, waiting for the next guest to arrive and the guest after that, and the next, staying true to my plan to arrive to a full house and not a moment sooner. It's now 8.15 and the doorbell continues to chime and through the door I hear the sound of my distinguished guests making their introductions. I follow the voices across the room to the central French doors and as I gingerly move the curtain to one side, I hear Doris Day discussing Act IV of *Swan Lake* with both Tchaikovsky and Matthew Bourne down on the terrace below. As I move away from the doors and adjust the weighty curtain I take one last glimpse down at the terrace, now lit with hundreds of breathtaking fairy lights that create a canopy under the silvery moonlight.

I poor myself a neat whisky on the rocks and I give in to the temptation of switching on the large screen that towers above the wall to the side of my bed. I sit with the remote control in my hand and cross my legs, resting my glass on my knee. The screen comes to life and the observation cameras work beautifully as I scan the sitting room in all its Victorian glory. The room is abuzz with light chatter and laughter and the piano is being played in the corner near to the terrace doors. The fireplace is glowing to provide ambiance more than heat and there is a light smoke in the air, which trails from the elegantly extended cigarette holder placed with such style in the corner of Tamar de Lempicka's mouth. There she is, as glamorous as one of her masterpieces. She has a beauty about her that I hadn't expected and a gravitation towards Michelangelo that I was absolutely expecting. Michelangelo looks more playful than accounts of his life would suggest and he has a warm but intense face. They stand in rapt conversation to the right of the fireplace and just behind them, sat on the grand piano in a world all of her own is Miss Monroe. My eyes widen as I hit zoom to take in every last inch of her beauty. She isn't talking to anyone, but moving her waist to the music and swaying her champagne glass around while daydreaming and firing her seductive features across the room in the direction of the main door. Her beauty isn't as I had imagined, there is softness to her face and a gentle unassuming innocence to her smile that quickly draws me in. I shake my stare and swiftly re-scan the camera to share her view. As I do, all the heads in the room turn in synchronicity with the camera and my guests start to curtsy as Oscar stands from the deep sofa to bow in the direction of the doorway. In the grandest of entrances, the room is engulfed with a different kind of aura, a majestic power that has commanded the attention of every eye. I fiddle for the controls to zoom out, and through the blinding light of the great hall Marie Antoinette glides in, dressed in her full feathered and hooped regalia, led by an exquisitely dressed Harvey Milk, who leads her delicate hand, albeit from behind, and in the shadow of her elegant profile. For a moment the air is tight and every hair on my body stands on end, just reacting to this fantastical moment. In the stillness, Marie Antoinette curtsies in recognition of the welcome from the fellow guests and as she recovers her posture, she dazzles the room with the most sincere, glittering smile. The room applauds and life resumes as the pianist starts to tap out a playful jazzy number, much to Miss Monroe's delight. I look away to the window and take a deep breath and then take another large gulp of whisky, now diluted by the reductive ice cube, that has fallen prey to the warmth of my hand. It's almost time.

I lift the jacket from its heavy hanger and ease myself into the pale grey fitted arms. I lean forward and smile into the illuminated dressing table mirror to check my teeth for whisky stains before adjusting my waistcoat to cover the edge of my slightly snug waistline. The excitement has turned to fear, but before I entertain the emotion the door is rapped three times and, ready or not, I know it's show time.

All sound disappears from my mind and a stillness engulfs the room as I turn to contemplate the now powerful and terrifying doorway. I move slowly, fighting the unmistakable signs of anxiety as my hand trembles as it reaches out for the handle. The consequential decision to pull the door open is immediate without any reluctance and all at once I am released from my momentary terror by a more overpowering emotion, the desire to be amongst them all, to see them all with my own eyes.

I walk along, what feels like, the never-ending landing, choosing to stay focused on what is in front of me while I fight every instinct to peer across the banister that is now the only barrier between me and my two party escorts for the evening. My legs tremble and my stomach surrenders into a circus of summersaults. This isn't first date nerves, this is a nervous breakdown all wrapped up in a few fleeting moments, a few fleeting moments that disappear when I reach the top of the staircase and time as I know it comes to a complete standstill. The clock chimes nine times and with each chime I make further progress down the staircase and into the grand marble hall. The hall is magnificent, with beautiful white marble pillars and a sweeping Victorian chequered floor that could easily be a grand ballroom in its own right. The space is beautifully lit by not one but three gloriously detailed glass chandeliers that shimmer and sparkle against each other and hover gracefully over the heads of my most special guests.

My left foot hits the hallway floor with a sharp clap, and then the right as I walk head down until we are face to face. I lift my head and smile right into Charlie Chaplin's eyes and he looks right back at me and smiles the most generous smile, before we grip each other like we are long lost friends finally reunited. I stand back and just stare at him. He isn't the tramp tonight; tonight he is dressed in a black top hat and tails and his beautiful energy washes over me in a moment of brilliance as I take in the view. I turn to the left and dressed in the identical suit and wearing it just as beautifully is my Lady Madonna. She smells like fresh flowers in spring and though steely in her posture, she has a vulnerability about her that is endearing. We don't hug but we look at each other and share a mutual smile that lasts for a short moment before she reaches out and takes my arm.

'So are we ready?' Madonna asks. 'I am now,' I reply and with a black-tied partner on each arm we walk through the sitting room and out onto the terrace where all of my guests are now assembled at the dinner table.

Everyone stands around the magnificent table that has been dressed with the purest white linen, the finest china and silverware that sparkles like diamonds in the moonlight. The flower displays reach up into the canopy of lights, a majestic array of roses, calla, antique lace and gardenia. Each and every guest has a glass raised in readiness for our arrival. I glance around feeling tears slowly rise in my eyes as I see Marsha P. Johnson and Silvia Rivera smiling right back at me. The toast isn't to me, the toast is to the occasion, the fantastical occasion of the Fantasy Dinner Party. I stop for a moment and before I let go of Madonna she leans towards me and says, 'Remember, nothing is ever truly what it seems.' 'I know,' I reply, 'but this is a fantasy and for now I am right here and so are you.' 'Well, if we are here, we may as well take our seats,' she suggests.

We take our places and I clear my throat to speak. 'Mesdames and Messieurs, it is my great privilege to have you here with me on this glorious evening, but before we toast love and wisdom, I must ask you all to consider a question so that you may also start to consider your answer. So, without much ado let us raise a glass to life, and as you take your seats, I ask you this, what is or what was the ultimate meaning of your life and more importantly, does it or did it set you free?'

The End

Je Ne Regrette Rien Part II

Anyway, back in the real world I had a real party to plan. Everything had to be perfect and I wouldn't let anyone help because I had to have control over every last aspect of the occasion – it was my party after all. I wasn't doing it just to have a party, to me it was a statement to myself that I had got to forty and I wasn't sorry about anything I had done to get there. I had no regrets and I wanted to celebrate the beginning of the next phase of my life with as many people as I could from the first half. I recognised that I had made decisions in life that led me down the road less travelled and everything I had ever experienced had got me to that room, that night, for that party with all of those beautiful people that meant so much to me. I had taken a hundred different paths, but they had all led me home that night, so how could any of them have been wrong? And of course at times some decisions felt like regrets, but those moments were fleeting, and I soon understood that that old cliché actually couldn't be truer – there really are no wrong decisions. Their blessings may not always bring instant enlightenment but they would always reward, teach, illuminate or prepare, like a good parent. In fact, for me the only wrong decision was indecision itself, the psychological prison of the naturally intrepid human mind. There is nothing comfortable to me about the suffocation of sitting on the proverbial fence. I would rather make a decision and jump, even if that means landing in a pile of freshly baked shit from time to time. I would rather that than risk getting the fence post stuck up my ass. The shit will eventually fall away as I make my way across the meadow, but I always remain less optimistic about the potential long-term damage of the fence post! Not that I haven't been guilty of fence sitting! William Blake once said, 'Hindsight is a wonderful thing, but foresight is better,' and to a point I agree, and as such I have a fair few fence post scars to show for it. However, when we truly engage with hindsight and learn from our past, only then do we develop the wisdom that leads to foresight. So maybe Blake's insight should read, 'Hindsight is an essential thing if we are to better ourselves with the wonder of foresight'. Eat your heart out Willy, I have a party to get to!

The night arrived and it was as perfect as I wanted it to be. The venue was a stylish nightclub in the centre of Cardiff and the room was decorated with black and silver balloons to match the black three-tier birthday cake and the silver stemmed champagne glasses that sat in readiness for the guests. The room was long and tall with a copper art deco style bar that overlooked soft velvet sofas that lined the walls in small booths.

With a few exceptions, everyone I wanted to be there were able to make it and it was such an amazing night. As I stepped onto the stage to do my thank you speech, the heavy drumbeats of 'Vogue' were pumping out from the speakers behind me. The room was dark but sparkling under the light of the glitter ball and the dance floor was full. I turned to face everyone and everything went into slow motion for a split second and as I scanned the room I realised how amazing it was to have so many wonderful people there. Flashes of faces that were no longer with us crossed my mind as I caught sight of the faces in the dark that were there, faces of people that whether they know it or not, I loved with all my heart. I have never ever really had a moment in my whole life when I remember feeling proud of myself, but in that second, I was proud, and as the butterflies flew away and as the music slowed, I smiled the sincerest smile I may have ever smiled and I started to speak.

In true Welsh style, my hopeful images of a mini party right out of the pages of *The Great Gatsby* evolved over the course of the night into drunken carnage. My personal highlight was Rhoda pretending to be Tina Turner while recruiting a whole stage of Tinas who trooped their way through 'Nutbush' with a certain amount of flair but very little composure. That was followed by the second highlight, which was watching a friend from Essex who happened to actually be called Tina slide sideways off her chair and onto the dance floor where she remained motionless for a few minutes before pulling herself together to take another large gulp of champagne. The extra mouthful of champagne was to steady herself, no doubt! I wasn't sure how the hell I had managed it, but I had got to forty and had marked the occasion with one hell of a party, beautiful friends, amazing family and in case I haven't already mentioned it, with absolutely no regrets. Je ne regrette rien.

Too soon the party was over and normality would soon resume. I couldn't escape my own question: 'What next?' Sometimes life suffocates you so that you can't think straight and you desperately look for a moment of peace, a place you can escape to, an empty space between the chaos where you can sit with yourself and breathe. I often imagined walking through a dense and aggressive forest but finding an opening to a sunlit meadow that would allow me to shed my skin and every expectation that was resting on my shoulders. Reaching forty was that time for me to escape from that forest, to shed the old and to make way for new, but before I moved on, I wanted just a little bit of time in the meadow, and maybe 2016 would be my meadow time. I had no clue what was beyond that meadow but I was more afraid of standing still than making my way forward to find out.

Blissfully Lost

I walk alone through the deep broken trees
The crackle of death breaks under my feet
The resilient green still alive on the breeze
The sun directing my path with its heat
Dragging my burden with desperate toil
Voices still twisting the knife to my cost
The chains of my making spill blood to the soil
No longer familiar, but not blissfully lost

In the distance a sparkle, a promise of dawn
A parting of darkness, a curious light
From the depths of the forest to life I am drawn
The magnificent wood now retreats from my sight
My heart starts to race with a plunder to move
My legs burst the lead that has crippled their pace
I scratch at the bark with something to prove
I stand at my gateway with God in my space

The dazzling beams of warmth soft and still
Wild flowers competing to capture my gaze
In the glorious meadow I'm captured at will
Like the songbirds that dart and dance in the haze
To the grass I surrender my body to lie
Caressed by the blades that feather my skin
Into the blue my eyes touch the sky
The deafening silence of peace without sin

Minutes and hours deliver their time
My body and spirit now weightless with love
In the break of a moment I see what is mine
Dispelling the blackness releasing the dove
In the beautiful nowhere is the place I am found
In the heavenly silence I hear secrets so loud
I am blissfully lost

I Am Wales

For some reason, I found leaving Wales so much harder the day after my party, harder than usual for sure. The car was driven to the front of the hotel and the hotel parking attendants started slowly loading my bags into the boot. I stood staring into the park across the road as the leaves twisted and tumbled from the trees, encouraged by the autumn wind that was picking up. I was grateful for the slow pace of the concierge who was now handing my keys over, and less grateful for the journey in front of me back to Essex. I didn't want to get in, and I am not sure I would have if not prompted. It wasn't the hangover of alcohol or emotions, but a deeper longing to stay, a steely desire to divert the car away from the M4 and up the A470 and into the valleys. I desperately wanted to lay on my parent's sofa and eat a Sunday roast made the way only my mam could make it. I was a Welsh boy through and through and sometimes I just needed to be home, and this was the moment I realised that visits were no longer enough. My body had been to many places all over the world and I had lived for many years in England, but my heart would always be only in one place. Inside my heart I was still the boy from the Welsh Valleys and a massive part of me will always want to be there with my mam and dad, my brothers Stuart and Geraint, my nieces and nephews and all of my amazing friends. I am so proud of where I am from, and the blood that runs through my veins will always be one hundred per cent Welsh, no matter where I am in the world. To me Wales really is God's country. It is beautiful, strong, poetic and humble and above all else, it is home.

More than anything else, most of the people I love most in this whole world are in Wales. They are my people and I am one of them. It is where I belong and Wales is very much part of who I am.

Whenever I travelled back into Wales I would always salute the giant flag that flies at the Celtic Manor Golf Resort as I drove past. I felt as though that flag was there to remind me that I was home. I probably looked a bit stupid, and sometimes an amused passenger in the outside lane would make a point of saluting back, which used to make me chuckle.

I knew that one day I would get in a car and make that journey across the bridge as a Welshman going home for good. I would drive past the all-engulfing comfort and wind-snapping beauty of the red dragon on the Celtic Manor flag and up though the emerald green valleys of the Rhondda and into the cosy warm welcome of No. 33 Aldergrove Road. Thirty-three Aldergrove Road, the place I was born, the place where I learned to feel brave, the place where I learned to feel loved, the place where I learned how to love, but most importantly, the place where my mam and dad sat patiently, waiting for me, always calling me home without ever having to say it out loud.

If I pass the Principality Rugby Stadium, I feel its energy bursting through the concrete pillars, when I hear the national anthem before a game I shed tears, and when I watch the rugby I feel the gut-wrenching pride of the dragon engulfing every part of me. If I hear a Welsh accent where I wouldn't expect to hear one, I have to say hello and if I hear someone say anything snide about Wales my walls fly up and I become the instant defender of my country. As the National Rugby tagline states, 'I Am Wales.' I am the walking, breathing proof that you can take the boy out of Wales but you will never ever take Wales out of the boy. Cymru Am Byth.

The Three-Feathered Prince

In the land of the songbird
I was born to the tune
A poet in blood
Not served with a spoon

From soft sooty cast
To mountains so loud
Sing voices of folk
So humble so proud

The harps in the valley
Play a song of the old
Underground treasure
The kingdom of gold

The emerald grass
Protecting her soil
The daffodil crown
Applauding her toil

To be like the dragon
Is not to breathe fire
But be tender of heart
To be strong, to inspire

The land of my mother,
My father, my race
The land that protects me
With beauty and grace

Though I roam from the path
From my staff and my throne
It's to Cymru Am Byth
I will always come home

I am not just a man
But a soul that prevails
The three-feathered prince
I am me, I am Wales

Wake-Up Call 2021

Five years have passed since the night I surrendered to my hotel bed, dizzy and dehydrated from the champagne excess of my fortieth birthday party. I don't know how I have landed here, but here I am and it is now July 2021 and five, nearly six years have almost vanished. It's a cloudy Friday evening and I am sat in the kitchen of my new house, on the outskirts of the Welsh Valleys. The daylight has started to subside and my attention flits from my laptop to the wine glass and out of the French windows and into the garden. The garden that has become my sanctuary in the last six months, the garden that I have watched grow from rugged nothingness and seed, to flourishing shape, colour and presence. I feel as though the very same garden has built its walls up around me, watching me, not grow but plateau. Sometimes watching me stumble, sometimes fall, but every now and then watching me rise, and in even more fleeting moments, watching me shine a little, but overall the balancing effect is best described as plateau. I feel as if I have almost woken up here in this moment after a long sleep, and I am now a million miles away from where I once was. The single wine glass and the silence reminds me that I am alone, independent, and yet more together and in control than I have ever been. It's one of those moments when the stillness settles around you and you start to hear the clock ticking, the ticking that stands to ground you into a semi state of hypnosis. Tik tok, tik tok, tik tok.

I have changed and life has changed. I spend more time gardening, walking and writing than I do at parties or on the dance podium. Life is in some ways easier now; it is somewhat secretly satisfying that I know the names of more garden shrubs and flower species than I do songs in the charts. I feel evolved, at peace with my path and yet still engulfed with a sense of even more evolution ahead. It isn't just me that has changed or is changing, the whole world has slightly adjusted, as it learns to live in the aftermath of Covid 19, a pandemic that really doesn't need any further introduction or explanation. Outside the garden walls, life is returning to an adjusted normality and the people I love have so far come through it unscathed. It's a strange moment, a strange evening and a strange week. The light outside has turned a few shades darker now and the clouds hang over the mountains casting mood-stealing shade. It's hard to tell if I am influencing the heavy, muggy, grey clouds or if they are influencing me. I take another sip of Sancerre, rest my head against the back of the sofa and close my eyes. I desperately search my heart and soul in a bid to make some sense of how the show-stealing headlines of Covid 19 and 'new normality' are slowly ebbing away, and yet in their departure they are pulling the dust sheets off of old enemies, enemies that we have spent less time fearing in the last eighteen months. As the news reporters search for new fear to pray on, they find old fear, fear more well-grounded and stubborn, fear that is going nowhere and fear that is still making new bloody ground.

The daily battles that run wild in my head have subsided and in this moment all I can think about is the loss of Samuel Luiz. I have taught myself to look for meaning and lessons in everything but I can't find the answers I have been searching for, for this. Samuel was a young twenty-four-year-old guy with the world at his feet and yet in an act of pure unprovoked horror, he was brutally beaten to death in Galicia, Spain by a group of homophobic men who chanted faggot over and over again, as they crushed his skull and bore down on his defenceless body until every ounce of life had been forced out. Samuel wouldn't have been the only gay man murdered during this week, but this was Spain, this was closer to home than I could have ever imagined and as wrong as it sounds, that has made it not just unfathomable, but so much worse. His life was no more important of course than the men and women murdered every day for the same crimeless crime, but Samuel was murdered in a country where progress had been made and freedoms had already been won. Samuel's murder had left me shaken by the realisation that there is still so much left to do, even in the places we celebrate liberation and equality.

I was at home after a longer than usual day at the office when I first sat down to read the story. Within seconds and only a few lines in, I felt tears trickle out of the corners of my eyes. I swiftly placed my phone on the coffee table in front of me and held my hands to my face, and with no control the trickle became a broken flood gate. I couldn't stop crying, I felt sick and I couldn't shake this immense feeling of hopelessness. Nothing had hurt more or touched me more since the morning I heard the news break on the Omar Mateen gun bloodbath in Florida. Both stories horrific in their own way and neither of them were about me, but they were brutal attacks on my community, my people, my brothers and sisters. They were attacks on every grieving mother and father, every war hero that had fought for our freedoms to be who we want to be, and they were attacks that glorified and magnified the hate and fear I thankfully only tasted as a child. If someone hurts my family, they hurt me, and if someone hurts my community, just because of who we are, then that also hurts me and triggers every devastating memory of being someone's gay target. A target to be dealt with, ridiculed and eradicated, all because our existence threatens a toxic society based on outdated masculinity. What would it take to tip the balance of society so that these minority groups of haters started to recognise the absurdity and irrelevance of their voices, as they shout across the street, 'walk like a man not a faggot,' or 'talk like a man, not a queer'? This week, in July 2021, I woke up, I had a wake-up call.

My belief that living out-loud, breeds tolerance had been tested. Yet, with the greatest confidence my resolve shifted up three gears. You see for me in between my tears for this beautiful young soul I grew a little, just like that day as a teenager, I cried for the young man on the TV dying with AIDS. I realised that for all my self-congratulation at coming out, somewhere in the darkness of the three previous days I had accepted the fact that I had more coming out to do, more truth to speak and more examples to set. I have become more convinced than ever, that the greatest tool we have to fight intolerance is to remove the fear, to expose over and over again a new norm, and therefore living our pure unadulterated truth out-loud, but for me louder, much louder than I ever had before.

As a child I wasn't just gay, I was gender fluid, I can see that now, but I was ashamed and conditioned by what was expected, what was tolerated and overwhelmed with just dealing with the main event which for me at the time, was the gay aspect. I am forty-five years old and it's taken this long for me to see that being gay was never the main event. I never wanted to be a girl, but I never saw myself as a 'proper' boy, I was a frustrated and often miserable child because I could not express myself the way I wanted to, based on feelings that I didn't belong in any of the boxes. I clip-clopped around the house in heels and blankets for dresses because I wanted to know what it felt like for a girl, not because I wanted to be one, but they got to express themselves with so much more freedom than boys did. Girls could wear shirts and trousers but to dress like a girl for a boy was forbidden, and that was hard to come to terms with when through your young eye's clothes had no gender. I was a feminine little human with so many amazing women as role models, I gravitated towards femininity and yet I thought it was wrong, I thought I was wrong, I thought I was broken. We didn't have non-binary or gender fluid back then, being undefined wasn't a thing and so it was transsexual, transvestite, gay, bi or straight. The honest truth was that I wasn't any of those things in isolation.

So I closed the door on who I was and conformed because who I was didn't exist, but I conformed in my own way, by my rules. If we had family shopping trips for big occasions, I would pick out the bright trousers and bold coloured shirts and jackets, I wore kilts for fashion whenever the opportunity presented itself and as I grew up I experimented with make-up in a very subtle way. I became satisfied that I could be me in my own way, and despite moments of my adult life where I have slipped back into full conformity, I have always let the true me come out in one way or another. It's taken forty-five years, but I am now done with being even a fraction less than the fullest version of who I am. My truth, is that I am gender fluid, based on how I feel on the inside, and I am learning to become more and more comfortable with how I present myself in this world. Would I look a little different had I been a young boy now in 2021? Probably yes, but I have found my way, and I owe it to myself and to those that follow, to come out, to be proud, and to live out loud. I am a gender fluid gay man, and it may not always appear that way, but for me the lion's share of how I identify has to do with how I feel. I have witnessed people being challenged and targeted for being non-binary or gender fluid and I have even witnessed the ridicule of people needing to self-identify from within the LGBTQ community. Until now I have always been an ally and active defender, and yet until now I have not come out and said, and this is also who I am. I still strive for a day where labels are unnecessary but that won't be in my lifetime, for now I am coming to terms with my deepest truth and yet in very simple terms I am just me and nothing about the person I am will ever really change. That is true of all of us, and I guess the fact that some people cannot see through it, is what hurts the most. Aside from the murder of Samuel Luiz, I had become increasingly inspired and moved to share my own truth because of the bravery and spectacular confidence of Fee, a good friend's brave and brilliant child. From a distance I had heard stories and read posts on the socials and observed with admiration as Fee made bold steps towards changing her life. In moments I have almost had to forgive myself for not being braver, stronger and more determined as a child, but my journey was different and I was different and I am okay with that. As for Fee, well Fee is a small human being who, at such a young age, has defied fear and expectation in living their life based on how they feel on the inside. A child that is supported by the most amazing, respectful, encouraging and evolved parents, and a child that in my view, is changing the world all on their own. A child that gives me hope of a brighter tomorrow, a child that should give us all hope while teaching the world a thing or two about life . If Fee can be Fee, then I am sure as hell that I can be me.

Soap Box Queen

Shine up that junk in your trunk and make some treasure

So, here we are. I have reached that age where the looking glass is clearer than ever before and the rose tinting that I had self-administered in my twenties, now has some cracks in it, shall we say. So yes, that brings with it the ability to see my own challenges, my ego and the not so pretty bits but hell, on the other hand I have so much self-respect now, and I see my own heart and you know what, it's not a bad one, it's good. I like being me, I like that I have opinions about everything, I like that I am more interested in breaking glass ceilings than polishing reflections. I am the strongest me I have ever been and I am okay with the battle scars that I carry. Without wanting to quote a great poem, I do absolutely carry them, I carry them in my growing heart. I hear the odd moment of defensiveness when I feel I am being challenged, I feel the paranoia rise up, when I feel that I am not liked and someone is going to attack me, and I still experience the moments of weakness when my demons remind me that I am only ever a life event away from being stolen by the crippling anxiety that has always left me feeling like a recovering addict. Most of all of the above is down to the fact that I was bullied, humiliated and made to feel like I was somehow a lesser human being! When you enter adulthood, you think you have escaped the trauma and you celebrate being free by just getting on with life, but the long-term impact of being bullied is like PTS, but a much slower burn. Before you know it, you recognise how it has shaped your view of the world and how you are forever changed because of the battles you fought to exist at such a young age. I don't want the violins to play by the way, I have accomplished a huge amount in my life, and I have so much to be grateful for and I have been blessed with so many opportunities, most of which I have seized, and I get all of that. I am cool with it all, I accept it all and, in some ways, I love it all, every last bit of it. It's my story and I eventually found my power in owning it.

So, with age comes experience they say, and with experience comes opinions, not that I have ever been short of them, so forgive my self-indulgence as I climb up onto my soapbox and share a little of my conclusions so far on this beautiful thing called life.

We all have the ability to make the very best of the gifts we have been presented with. We shouldn't pretend that the obstacles we are dealing with are nothing, but we should face our saboteurs and refuse to let them define us. So yes, I was gifted the queen's crown, I was born feeling like my gender could be defined within the margins of gender binary, and no nurture would have ever changed me. Being different is finally accepted in a significant percentage of the world, but growing up it wasn't easy and I always felt the weight of how I identified resting heavily on my shoulders, both as a teenager and sadly at many points during my adult life. I have been isolated in business environments because I couldn't talk about being one of the lads at the football on the weekend, I have had to correct hundreds of people over the years who make assumptions and start referring to my partner as girlfriend or wife, I have watched grown people squirm and struggle to respond when they find out, wanting so desperately to let me know that it's okay with them. I mean, it's okay with them? How do people still get to say that? How is it okay for someone to declare that my existence is okay with them! Why should they get the privilege of giving me their approval? So yes, it's not always dramatic, or wrapped up in an active assault, but I still live with discrimination. The only difference is that I have now learned not to explain myself, ever. I never declare anything about myself that places me into someone else's neat little box, and I never give anyone the power to tell me it's okay! If someone tells me, 'It's okay, I am cool with it,' my response is now always, 'Oh, I'm sorry, you must be confused because that sounded like an answer, and I never asked a question.' Our approval is self-owned and one hundred per cent self-perpetuating.

So yes, I have felt oppression and intolerance and I have had to go into battle with myself to wake up to the opportunity of being the real me. Nobody gave me lemons to make lemonade, but I was repeatedly called a 'queen' and a 'queer' at school, not only bullied for being gay, but being reminded that being gay in society equalled being weak, lesser than, an outcast and a freak. One day when I was at my lowest, something momentary but life changing happened. A few of the boys had made an ugly black paper crown and had sneaked up on me from behind in the class of a teacher who had little to no control. The boys managed to force the crown onto my head, to the erupting amusement of most of the other kids. I ran from the class, failing to pull the crown from my head until I go to the isolation of the boys' toilets. Staring in the mirror, I saw the word queen staring back at me, emblazoned on the crown in perfectly cut paper letters. I didn't cry – I'd become tired of doing that. What I had was more of a gentle epiphany. That moment of not being able to take any more abuse woke a strength somewhere from deep inside and I started to change, only a little but enough to begin an inner revolution that would last way into adulthood. I decided that if I have to own that name, that brand, like a crown, then I was going to polish that ugly, twisted crown right up. That crown was going to be so bright that the haters would be blinded by its very existence! I was going to polish that crown and make the world see that it wasn't just okay to be me, it was more than that – it was a privilege, a blessing, a gift and something to aspire to. I had taken control, and since that moment I was able to tap into my innate capacity to share my truth and to let the small world around me to see me for who I really was with love and without fear. The cliché that tells us that you have to love yourself before you can truly love anyone else, well, whoever came up with that was onto something because I am telling you, that is the God damn truth!

I want *Polish The Crown* to be more than just a book to those that may read it; I want it to be an invitation for people to not just face their fears but to walk straight through them. I want people to talk and write about overcoming the grey and finding the colour. I want people to write about their extraordinary lives and in doing so to encourage change and inspiration. I want people to take what others think is just acceptable and push the buttons required to challenge those belief systems. If you're standing on a high plateau, you might think the mountain below you is no big deal, but that's not true for the people still climbing it. Remember this, we don't climb the mountain to become the view, we conquer that damn mountain to experience the view, so throw a rope to those who still need help to get there. More than half of the world is still climbing that mountain to tolerance and freedom and too big a percentage of those haven't even got the means to start the journey. I want people to embrace who they are and to take ownership for the ultimate responsibility we all have to make ourselves happy. We owe it to the world and all those we love, to believe in ourselves, because only then can we reach our true potential and start the butterfly effect of making that belief contagious. Only when we are happy can we truly enable ourselves to help others. It's pure logic: you can't share what you haven't got. You don't have to be Marsha P. Johnson, Silvia Rivera or Patrick Trevor-Roper and you don't have to march in the streets to fight for your freedom (unless you want to!), you can start a revolution of love simply by finding your peace with being you, just like I have done in the last few months. In being you completely and unapologetically, you teach the world around you what tolerance and acceptance is, and that small step will help the journey of educating the world until we have acceptance without exception.

So pick up your crown and polish that shit right up, make it matter, make it stand out and most of all and most importantly, remember if and only if that crown fits, don't fight it, but be it!

'Once when I was looking down, an ugly crown was placed upon my head and I was branded a queen. I used my tears to polish that crown up until it shimmered, until it sparkled, until I defined it. Now I wear that crown in spirit, in power and in pride, and never will I look down again.'

Rise for a Nirvana and only settle for heart shaped freedom

Labels are essential right now in breaking down walls and building identify, empowerment and a sense of expression, but we must not settle for this as the ultimate end game. We could continue to create new labels and definitions of who we are every day, and that process would simply serve to compound what makes us different as a human race. News flash, we are all unique from the moment we are conceived, it's just at a much deeper, spiritual level than the way we present ourselves on the outside. If human beings are to evolve to a state of boundless equality, then we must accept that we are born individual and the nature of that individuality can finally only be defined by the nature of our soul. The garish, restraining view that skin, age, sexuality or body parts make us who we are or how we behave must one day be dismissed. The view that our choice of partner or choice of self-expression is lesser if it's choice over nature, needs to become irrelevant. We are not gay, we are not old, we are not trans, we are not androgynous, we are not straight and we are not a penis or a pair of breasts. We are a civilisation of spiritual beings, we are soul, compassion, love and purpose and the day we strive for the irrelevance of our self-limiting labels is the day we transcend to a new evolution of humanity!

That does not mean that we never look back with respect, honour and love for the movements, freedom fighters and necessary labels that one day will become a historic past. Instead, it means that we pay tribute to that past by never settling for anything less than the continuous, relentless progress of the human revolution of life and the onward fight for the ultimate human goal of optimum existence.

Let us not stop until we have freedom without fear, expression without the need for acceptance, love without persecution and peace without war. To start this revolution, we must start inside of our own minds, we must navigate beyond all we have learned and re-train or unlearn. For those of us on that path, we must keep going. For those that are ready to start then you must begin the journey, and for those that are lying to themselves that they are already there then it's time to close your eyes and ears and begin to see and listen with your heart. Nobody is immune to the system, we are all defined by society, exposed and paraded as subcategories of life in a bid to control us and separate us. Black, white, straight, gay, old, young, penis, vagina.

Until the day twelve-year-old Harry can just decide to change their name to Harriet, until the day a mother can buy her teenage son a dress because that's how he wants to express himself at the school party, until the day the fifty-five-year-old married father of two and CEO can walk into the boardroom in a three-piece suit, lipstick and matching heels, until the day the seventy-five-year-old mother of four can meet and marry the first lady she ever loved in a Catholic church, until the day an African American president can take office with her female lover as first lady, until that day we have a revolution to continue, because if you can say in your deepest truth that those things today could be without ridicule, chaos or persecution then you are lost, and I don't believe that any of us are ever really lost.

Peace and universal tolerance are states that can only ever be achieved and truly celebrated when they are available to all of us, to every human being in every geographical corner of our planet. Until we embrace the world like a loving mother would her children, we won't win. We must fight for peace for the world like a mother would fight for her children's safety, we must persevere and not bask for too long in the wins along the way, we must not become side-tracked by progress. We must continue the fight like the mother of two who saved one drowning child and would continue to give her life until both her children were back safe in the boat. We are all parents now, we are all empowered to design the future and all we have to do to start that revolution is to start with how we see the world through our own eyes. Once we see the world as a community we start to learn new behaviour, we learn to fight our own learned impulses to be reactive to what makes us different. Finally, we start to change the world the day we accept everything, because we realise that acceptance was never required in the first place. As freedom fighters of life our ambitions must become bigger, and the voices of ultimate equality must get louder until we achieve freedom not just for some, but for all of us.

And breathe…

In the here and now I am in a place where my creative blood has started flowing again and I have a deep desire to write and to keep fighting for our freedoms, whatever that looks like. I wrote this book in dedication to those that have gone before me and who have won my freedom. I also wrote this book for those that have still to win that freedom and in many ways I hope that this book itself becomes a mini freedom fighter. I hope that if the odd friend or relative does take the time to read it they will see how they have touched and changed my very normal life and I hope they will realise how much I love them.

I have everything I will ever need already surrounding me and I am exactly where I was always meant to be right in this very moment. I am here because I have always ruled myself. I made my own mistakes, my own choices and have always done things my way, no matter what the world around me has expected. I used to think I was an androgynous gay man who publicly toed the line to make others feel comfortable. Now I see clearly, like I did when I was a child, and what I am is a human being with boundless potential to be and to express myself in any way I see fit because I have woken up to the necessity to live my truth. I carry with me a responsibility to be me and to be me proudly, because I realise I bring nothing to the revolution that is life if I pretend to be anything less than what I see my everything to be.

We make a difference simply by being born. By just existing we affect the lives of those around us, but when we grow up we have a choice; we can decide whether to make a positive difference or not. I try my hardest to make a positive difference to the tiny space I occupy and for the people that occupy that space with me.

As for my tomorrow, well that's a whole different story. Life is not always perfect and yet I am cursed with always wanting and sometimes expecting it to be – that is who I am. I was born with great expectations and I will never change. For every disappointment there is a moment of perfection and those moments are always worth waiting for, especially if the small steps start to create change. People say they can't change the world, but they fail miserably to see the bigger picture, because all we have ever had to do was to change the world around us. The butterflies do the rest.

Fantastical Destiny

I travel under a canopy of dreams, being seduced by the glass ceiling of limitation that invites me to explode through its boundaries, trailblazing my truest purpose and my highest potential.

My canopy is made of the grandest, most enchanted array of autumn leaves. The leaves sleep cheek-to-cheek, conducting shade and light into my world in glorious reds, browns, yellows and rust.

I am gliding under my beautiful mysterious canopy, levitating above the earth, travelling through my space, observing my desire to climb, dismissing the self-made chains of reality that tease my choice, that gently dance to control my gravitation towards what I know to be my truth.

The leaves conspire to create the darkest shade to remind me of my primitive state in a heavenly sent ambition to stir my passion for what could be.

The leaves lift and flutter in a fleeting moment, letting in a piercing ray of the most dazzling light to confirm the glorious reward of my life's curiosity.

My feather-light spirit reaches out its innocent hands to feel the warmth of my passion, encouraging the weight of my body to ascend from the icy frost of contentment.

I stare, I admire, I welcome in the sun and I give my body to the dream of the greatest love, to the light that can never be unseen, I smile through the tears of my spurious loss and surrender to my fantastical destiny.

The desire to keep searching for more, for happiness, will always exist in me. I'm not sure I know what happiness really is, but I know I have experienced it many times. Maybe it isn't a destination but moments of light in the shade. After all, if it weren't for the shade, how would we recognise the light, right? Either way, I am certain of one thing about happiness, and that is we all have a responsibility to find it. I started this short book with 'Little Leaf', a poem I wrote about my fear of letting go of what was holding me back and I finish this book with my final poem, 'Beautiful Drum', which is about reconnecting with life and self-belief. Since starting this project I have felt passion in my hands as they have glided across the laptop keys and I have drawn tears to my own eyes with reflections of the past. I have written lines that have touched me almost as if they were being written through me. This book has been one of the greatest life review periods I have ever experienced, it's become a friend and a link to the past that is so easily forgotten. I have cherished this time and will always look back on these pages and feel the warmth they gave me as I was writing them. My wish is that one day these pages will inspire another to write an account of their beautiful, extraordinary life, and in many future generations from now there will be a catalogue of real stories that tell the tales of many wonderful human spirits that eventually changed the world because they all started mini revolutions of love in their refusal to accept anything less than freedom.

I couldn't finish this work without taking the time to write a letter to my younger self, a young boy who I had forgotten and unfortunately a young boy I have taken far too long to acknowledge my respect for. So this one is for mini-me.

Hey You,

You don't know me but I know you very well. I have always known you, but I just haven't had the time to think about you very much lately, and I'm sorry about that. Perhaps I should explain a little better. You see, you and I are old friends. We did everything together. I was there for your first cardboard washing machine, your first performance of 'Like a Virgin' on the hallway floor, I was there the first time you dared to dream, I was there for your first kiss, the first time someone hurt you, the first time you cried yourself to sleep because you were scared of life and I was there when you first realised you fancied Mark Owen from Take That and Madonna not so much ☺*. You thought you were messed up, you thought you were broken, you thought you were not worthy of much, you actually thought that you were far too average at everything to be anything. I have news for you: you will never be average, you will always be worthy of everything you ever want. So you are a little bit messed up, that bit may be true, but hey what kid isn't? And none of it is your fault. You carry the world on those little shoulders, feeding off everyone else's problems and struggles. Please try not to. As you grow you will realise that there is a difference between taking ownership of life and taking ownership of your life. Please try to learn as soon as you can that taking ownership of your life is about owning the things that you can influence, and that is the only ownership you can take. Let go of what you cannot change, because in changing what you can, you will change the world anyway.*

You don't have a hard life so there is no point in pretending that you do. You have everything you have ever asked for and you have parents that love you completely. You are a pain in the ass sometimes and you speak before thinking and have temper tantrums if things didn't go your way but you love deeply, and that is why it is always so easy for anyone to hurt you and often for you to hurt yourself. By the way, the speaking without thinking thing doesn't really go away, but as you get older they will call it having an opinion, which is a green light in my book… Remember everyone is entitled to your opinion so never stop expressing yourself.

You are a dreamer; you look at the world like a child opening a beautifully wrapped gift on Christmas morning. You were born awestruck by all that life has to offer, even if it sometimes frightens you. You want to be a singer, a dancer, an actor, an architect, a journalist, the prime minister, and you want to write beautiful poetry, well keep dreaming because you can be any and all of those things, but let your instinct in, trust it and let it lead you. You doubt yourself sometimes because people have doubted you. You don't need to ever doubt yourself, and deep down you have a certainty that you can achieve anything you set your mind to. As you grow up you will learn to turn others' negativity into fuel for your fire and you will make it a mission of yours to prove the haters and non-believers wrong.

You have a few sayings that you live your life by, 'Don't wait for someone to perform with' was the one that I remember most. I wish I could help you understand what that means right now, but it's a good mantra so stick with it, because it is so very true. You will never need anyone to help you find your way in the world. In many moments of your life you will be the bird on the tree branch confused and terrified that the branch will fall away. Just so you know, one day you will realise that the little bird never needed the branch because it already had wings to fly. You will grow fiercely independent, determined to stand alone. People you love will sometimes confuse that with you not needing them, it will be up to you to make sure they know, that you still do.

I have another apology to make. I'm sorry that I rug-swept the days that you cried into your pillow to hide the noise, the days when you couldn't sleep in fear of going to school. I'm sorry I have forgotten how brave you are and how much you helped me be me today. I'm so proud of how you look after yourself and make yourself and everyone around you think it is no big deal. I know it is a big deal, I know how much you are hurting and I wish you would ask for help, but you won't, I know you won't because I know your heart.

Now for some advice, albeit a bit late and beside the point. Stop worrying about your hair and your skinny waist! I mean really? Your hair will eventually fall out after years of very expensive trips to Toni & Guy and your waist well, that will expand without any real effort on your part until one cruel day you will have lost the one you had all together, never to be seen again. Don't worry what people think. So you can do nearly every Madonna dance move and you enjoy it, so what? Just a little tip: your brother has watched you doing your dance thing plenty of times through the lounge window and you are so in the zone, you will never realise. In fact he will tell you one day that not only did he see you through the window but he thought you were pretty good ☺. Oh and though you really won't believe it now, one day when you sample alcohol you will get drunk and Vogue on club podiums in London & New York to a packed crowd, at weddings and in bars all over the world and amazingly you won't give a flying hoot what anyone thinks. To top off not giving a hoot, sometimes you will be cheered and applauded for it. Yes, I understand that bit is a bit of a pill to swallow... but true I promise.

Don't worry about not being the most popular boy in the class or about your general confidence and likability. You will learn that people confuse confidence with ego. Being certain that you are liked by everyone is ego. Being certain that you'll be absolutely fine if you're liked or not, is confidence. One day you will have that in good measure and nobody will take it away from you – although be prepared for a few people to try.

You worry too much, please stop it. Enjoy your scatty, overly ambitious energy and never be anything else but you and be you well. Kiss the girls, kiss the boys, wear the dress, wear the trousers, work hard and relax your busy mind once in a while. Most of all and most importantly, never stop trusting your instinct. You always had it finely tuned and you should never every forget to trust it because it will be your greatest asset.

You're okay, you know. You are more than okay – you're fucking amazing and unique, and in your own way you will set your world on fire. I love you xxx

Beautiful Drum

Life, so much more than a show, a performance or circus
A tale to be lived, be uncaged, be amorphous
Be silly, be playful, be crazy, be fun
Little one, hear the beating of your beautiful drum
Let the world feel the rhythm of your beautiful drum

Let no being bring shadow or night to your day
Find your shine in your spirit, your dazzling ray
The whisper of love that says you're the one
Precious one, hear the beating of your beautiful drum
Let the world feel the rhythm of your beautiful drum

In confusion and doubt find the heart just to be
Look inside to your truth and then you will see
In your uniqueness your river of courage will run
Fearless one, hear the beating of your beautiful drum
Let the world feel the rhythm of your beautiful drum

Be as free as the air, like the wind you should dance
Use your voice to cast kindness, giving a rainbows a chance
Be the rebel of peace, fight for freedoms not won
Courageous one, hear the beating of your beautiful drum
Let the world feel the rhythm of your beautiful drum

In the chaos seek silence, let the still be your guide
But don't stand at the back, seize your place, come alive
Be your glorious colours, know your strength and become
Boundless one, hear the beating of your beautiful drum
Let the world feel the rhythm of your beautiful drum

Be the wild and untamed, the maverick unbound
Never fit in the box that will lose what you've found
Let your heart drive out darkness, never fire the gun
Peaceful one, hear the beating of your beautiful drum
Let the world feel the rhythm of your beautiful drum

Be you, only you, find your power in that
Share yourself bare your soul, wear a crown for a hat
You are all of your blessings you're the whole, you're the sum
Special one, hear the beating of your beautiful drum
Let the world feel the rhythm of your beautiful drum

With wisdom, with pride see the love at your side
All the spectacular spirits who are sharing your ride
Be a brother, a mother, a sister, a son
Beautiful one, hear the beating of your beautiful drum
Let the world feel the rhythm of your beautiful drum
Shine so bright. Be the moon, be the stars, be the sun

Grand Exit

There, I am done; my little journey is over, so from the beginnings I will give you the end – but not before my grand exit. Brace yourself it's going to be a bit, what I like to call, rainbow dramatic and God knows we all need a bit of rainbow dramatic to brighten our world!

Picture the scene: it's midnight and I write my last line as the clock chimes 12. I throw down my elegant Montblanc ink pen, before pushing myself away from the walnut desk with a force that sends me spiraling backwards in celebratory self-congratulation along the polished oak floorboards of my private study. I stand slowly, creating an air of anticipation in the dimly lit room and start to turn my face towards the darkness of the towering doorway. With a sudden twist of old Hollywood movie magic, the interior walls diminish and I am standing atop a gloriously grand gilt staircase that cascades opulently onto the marble hallway of the decaying but still lavish mansion on Sunset. I turn to face the crowd of police that have come to arrest me for the murder of my estranged lover. My eyes are wide open and I stare intensely through my now-crazy hair.

I know what you're thinking, and stop being a clever dick and just humor me. In this scene I have hair okay!

Right, where were we – yes! So, I stare intensely through my crazy, mangled hair, which has fallen over my somewhat ravaged but still youthful face. As the gathering reporters start to flash their cameras and extend their zoom lenses, from within my tormented frown I start to smile. Not a friendly sort of smile, but more of a horror film 'I am going to kill you, because I can and I am crazy person' type of smile. I swish a ridiculously heavy Shirley Bassey style feather cape from around my shoulders and drop it to the dusty floor revealing my part gothic ball gown, part tuxedo ensemble. I adjust my black top hat and reach for my diamond encrusted cane as my blood red dragon's tail swings out of confinement to rest front and center, at my feet. There I stand undefined, unapologetic, unstoppable, applauded by the slow but powerful melody of the dark haunting piano that has started to play. Every window bursts open and the wind of ten gales enters the house, engulfing every room and sending every curtain dancing into the air, unveiling the misty but graceful sunset that is now calling my name. I stand, I still stand, despite everything and because of everything I still stand. I raise my hands to the ceiling like Evita about to address Argentina and with a firm but gentle tone I speak, 'You see, this is my life. It always will be! There's nothing else – just us – and this book – and those wonderful lights out there in the dark. I am ready, I give in, I surrender to my fate, to my crown and I am finally ready for my close-up.'

Lights flash in a majestic frenzy as the orchestra reaches a magnificent crescendo and a thousand glitter guns fire their rainbow consignment of love, smothering the crowd, who now feel the vibrations of the marching drumbeats applaud under their feet, louder and louder and louder and louder... I cry out, 'This cannot be the end, this can only be the end of the beginning,' and it was!

Acknowledgments

I acknowledge all of the people who have touched my life in so many beautiful ways, from my best friends, partners, and my beloved family. I have a story to tell because of those that have loved me and fuelled my confidence in being me as fully and as loudly as I can be.

I also have to acknowledge the mesmerising talents of Barbara Ana Gomez, who has taken my concepts. my poetry and some terrible draft drawings, and created the most beautiful collection of illustrations. I am genuinely forever in your debt. You made this experience a thrill, and I will never forget the excitement I felt, every time a new illustration appeared in my inbox. You are so talented and I am so lucky that you agreed to work with me, thank you.

I specifically have to acknowledge those closest to me over the last five years, for their encouragement, patience and interest in what it was that I was creating. Matt, Sarah (AKA Sazzle), Jonathan (AKA Rhoda) and Bette. You may never realise it, but your support has fuelled me to get this project over the finish line, and I love you all.

Finally, I have to thank two special people who inspired me, to not only write an account of my memories, but two people who inspire me to be brave and to live my best life everyday. My wonderful parents, I love you both more than you will ever know.

About the Author

Christopher Anstee is a self-proclaimed poet and writer who lives on the outskirts of the Rhondda Valleys in South Wales. A profound soul searcher and theologian, Christopher is the archetypal daydreamer, always contemplating and searching for the change and colour in life, and never satisfied with the greyness of the status quo.

A lover of words and images, Christopher is deep rooted in his country of birth and feeds off the land, history and spiritual energy of Wales, in all it's beautiful unboastful mystery. That said, adventure and travel has been as important in his life, as the place he calls home. Like Wales, some of Christopher's favourite places in the world are places steeped in history, mystery or pure natural beauty, such as Banff, Venice and San Francisco.

Christopher has developed not only a passion for LGBTQ+ equality, but a passion for challenging the stereotypes of this world, including the deconstruction of outdated masculinity and the concept of clothes having the power to define gender.

Underneath his passions and beliefs, Christopher is a 46 year old gay man who loves family, gardening, poetry, friends and a glass or six of a good Sancerre. Sometimes vulnerable, sometimes fiery and sometimes just bloody hard work, Christopher is a lover of life, art and self-expression. A traveller, a poet and a dreamer, always searching for adventure and love; hopeful that one day he will be the eccentric man down the street with a thousand books, 5 dogs and a million stories.

Printed in Great Britain
by Amazon

86987796R00120